JUN 3 1 1985

W9-BEX-497

143017

X
549
Ba

Bancroft
World's finest minerals and crystal

MEDIA SERVICES
EVANSTON TOWNSHIP HIGH SCHOOL
EVANSTON, ILLINOIS 60204

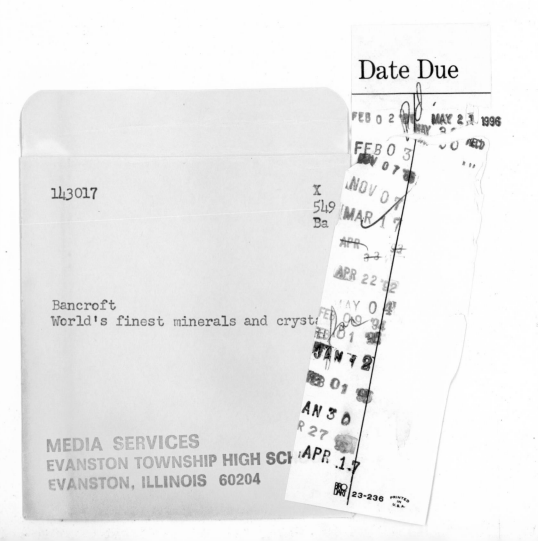

Date Due

FEB 0 2   MAY 2 1 1996

FEB 0 3

NOV 07

MAR 1 7

APR

APR 22

MAY 0 4

FEB

FEB 0 1

JAN 1 2

FEB 01

AN 3 0

R 27

APR 1 7

BRO
DART 23-236 PRINTED IN U.S.A.

The World's Finest
MINERALS and CRYSTALS

The World's Finest
MINERALS and CRYSTALS

by Peter Bancroft

A Studio Book
THE VIKING PRESS
New York

MEDIA SERVICES
EVANSTON TOWNSHIP HIGH SCHOOL
EVANSTON, ILLINOIS 60204

Copyright 1973 in all countries of the International Copyright
Union by Peter Bancroft
All rights reserved
First published in 1973 by The Viking Press, Inc.
625 Madison Avenue, New York, N.Y. 10022
Published simultaneously in Canada by
The Macmillan Company of Canada Limited
SBN 670-79022-2
Library of Congress catalog card number: 77-186742
Printed in France by Draeger, Paris

X
549
Ba

28.50

1/23/79

CONTENTS

143017

PANEL OF JUDGES AND CONSULTANTS

These are the distinguished experts who were instrumental in suggesting, judging, and selecting the minerals and crystals included in the Plates that make up the Gallery of this book.

PIERRE BARIAND, *Curator, Faculty of Sciences, Sorbonne, Paris* ★ G. P. BARSANOV, *Director, Fersman Mineralogical Museum, Moscow,* U. S. S. R. ★ GERHARD BECKER, *dealer, Idar-Oberstein,* WEST GERMANY ★ BONA POTENZA BIANCHI, *Curator, University of Milan, Institute of Mineralogy Museum, Milan,* ITALY ★ DRAGA BLOGOJEVIC, *geologist, Trepca,* YUGOSLAVIA ★ OLIVER CHALMERS, *Curator, Australian Museum, Sydney,* AUSTRALIA ★ ROCK CURRIER, *photographer and collector, Ardsley, New York,* U. S. A. ★ WALTER CURVELLO, *Curator, National Museum, Rio de Janeiro,* BRAZIL ★ J. DELORME, *mineral dealer, Tananarive,* MALAGASY REPUBLIC ★ VINCENZO DE MICHELE, *Curator, Civic Museum of Natural History, Milan,* ITALY ★ PAUL DESAUTELS, *Curator, Smithsonian Institution, Washington, D.C.,* U. S. A. ★ PETER EMBREY, *Curator, British Museum (Natural History), London,* ENGLAND ★ CLIFFORD FRONDEL, *Curator, Harvard University, Cambridge, Massachusetts,* U. S. A. ★ JOAQUIN FOLCH GIRONA, *Curator, private museum, Barcelona,* SPAIN ★ EDWARD GUBELIN, *collector and jeweler, Lucerne,* SWITZERLAND ★ CLAUDE GUILLEMIN, *Director, National Geological Service, Orleans,* FRANCE; *Curator, School of Mines, Paris* ★ F. HOFMANN, *Professor, School of Mines, Freiberg,* EAST GERMANY ★ GEORGE HOLLOWAY, *collector, Northridge, California,* U. S. A. ★ CORNELIUS HURLBUT, *Professor, Harvard University, Cambridge, Massachusetts,* U. S. A. ★ AKIRA KATO, *Curator, National Science University Museum, Tokyo,* JAPAN ★ CHARLES KEY, *dealer, St. Petersburg, Florida,* U. S. A. ★ HUGH LEIPER (*deceased*), *Editor,* Lapidary Journal, *San Diego, California,* U. S. A. ★ ORLOV LEONIDOVICH, *Secretary, Fersman Mineralogical Museum, Moscow,* U. S. S. R. ★ VINCENT MANSON, *Chairman, Department of Mineralogy, American Museum of Natural History, New York, New York,* U. S. A. ★ V. C. MEEN (*deceased*), *Chief Mineralogist, Royal Ontario Museum, Ontario,* CANADA ★ THOMAS MCKEE, *collector, Paradise Valley, Arizona,* U. S. A. ★ HENRICH NEUMANN, *Curator, Geology Museum, Oslo,* NORWAY ★ OLE V. PETERSEN, *Curator, Mineralogy Museum, University of Copenhagen,* DENMARK ★ TH. SAHAMA, *Professor, University of Helsinki, Helsinki,* FINLAND ★ WILHELM SCHILLY, *Professor, Mineralogical Institute, Bonn,* WEST GERMANY ★ H. J. SCHUBNEL, *Professor and author, School of Mines, Paris,* FRANCE ★ JOHN SINKANKAS, *author and collector, San Diego, California,* U. S. A. ★ H. A. STALDER, *Curator, National History Museum, Bern,* SWITZERLAND ★ JAROSLAV SVENEK, *Professor, National Museum, Prague,* CZECHOSLOVAKIA ★ EDWARD SWOBODA, *wholesale jeweler and collector, Los Angeles, California,* U. S. A. ★ RALPH TOWNSEND, *Curator, Geological Museum, Johannesburg,* SOUTH AFRICA ★ MAX WIEBEL, *Professor, Swiss Federal Institute of Technology, Zurich,* SWITZERLAND ★ DAVID WILBER, *dealer and collector, Reno, Nevada,* U. S. A ★ C. DOUGLAS WOODHOUSE, *Professor, University of California, Santa Barbara, California,* U. S. A. ★ **ALSO** ★ EDWIN ALLABOUGH, *collector, Cathedral City, California,* U. S A. ★ EDWARD BANCROFT, *collector, San Diego, California,* U. S. A. ★ WERNER BURGER, *collector, Zurich,* SWITZERLAND ★ FRED CASSIRER, *collector, New York, New York,* U. S. A. ★ ALBERT CHAPMAN, *collector, Sydney,* AUSTRALIA ★ M. DUSTERUD, *Museum Manager, Mining Museum, Kongsberg,* NORWAY ★ PAUL FRAENKEL, *collector, Paris,* FRANCE ★ JOHN FULLER, *Mineral Assistant, British Museum (Natural History), London,* ENGLAND ★ E. M. GUNNELL, *collector, Denver, Colorado,* U. S. A. ★ HENRI HANSON, *photographer and collector, Ardsley, New York,* U. S. A. ★ AVO HARNIK, *Curator, Swiss Federal Institute of Technology, Zurich,* SWITZERLAND ★ JOHN JAGO, *collector, San Francisco, California,* U. S. A. ★ ALAN JOBBINS, *Curator, Geological Museum, London,* ENGLAND ★ LOUIS MOYD, *Chief, Mineral Division, National Museum of Natural Sciences, Ottawa,* CANADA ★ LIVIA ÖRKÉNYI, *Chief Mineralogist, Hungarian Natural History Museum, Budapest,* HUNGARY ★ GEORGE PICK (*deceased*), *geologist, Lima,* PERU ★ SYDNEY PIETERS, *dealer and collector, Windhoek,* SOUTH-WEST AFRICA ★ KAREL TUCEK, *Director of Minerals, National Museum, Prague,* CZECHOSLOVAKIA ★ ERIC WELIN, *Curator, Royal Museum of Natural History, Stockholm,* SWEDEN ★

INTRODUCTION

For the lover of minerals, the Gallery section of this book presents a unique experience; for the first time he can enjoy an array of seventy-eight specimens each judged best of its species or type of the more than two thousand species and their varieties in the mineral kingdom. But what sensational specimens the seventy-eight are! The judges and consultants believe that the Gallery collection represents the finest group of minerals and gems ever photographed. It is hoped that you, the reader, concur.

This volume was never intended to be merely a picture book or a scientific journal. Rather, the continuous objective was to search out and photograph some of the best minerals in the world. A number of the minerals shown are very rare; quite a few are illustrated here for the first time.

Although collecting and cutting minerals and gems is now one of the largest and fastest-growing hobbies in the world, there is no known standard for measuring the quality of minerals; this volume, therefore, may perhaps serve as a bench mark in this area.

A special element in the production of this volume was the involvement of hundreds of collectors, dealers, curators, art buffs, and rock hounds who nominated specimens for review or served as judges and so became, in fact, co-authors of the book.

Certainly one of the greatest thrills for the author was his good fortune in meeting the many talented, friendly, and helpful people who formed the supporting cadre without whose help this project could not have been completed.

By 1965 the author had logged more than 250,000 miles in searching for outstanding minerals, in discussing classic specimens with curators and collectors, and in contacting recognized crystal photographers. Another quarter of a million miles and six more years were to elapse before the project would be completed.

As a beginning, a list was compiled of 150 species and types of minerals that would be of most interest to the collector, curator, and layman alike. Some items qualified because they nearly always appear as beautiful crystals. Others were selected for rarity, and a few were chosen because they are basic or rock-forming minerals of the mountains about us. This list was mailed to hundreds of mineral societies and to all important mineralogical museums, and was published twice in the *Lapidary Journal*. Hundreds of nominations were received from all over the world. The most frequently recommended mineral—predictably—was white quartz (rock crystal).

It was obvious that any selective factors used in choosing the finest of the minerals would be subjective at best. No known scientific formula distinguishes one "good" specimen from another, so as many experts as possible were involved in the nomination and selection process. The list of judges and consultants constitutes a great portion of today's experts. Among them are authors, collectors, dealers, cutters, curators, scientists, professors, geologists, and gem experts from almost every major country. Their collective knowledge about quality display specimens is enormous. These experts reviewed slides, photographs, and any other available data. Extreme care was exercised to insure that they were judging the mineral and not the photograph, and trick photography was disqualified. Some of the judges submitted personal lists of nominations, but if a judge's or consultant's own mineral had been nominated, he was not permitted to vote for his specimen. Occasionally there was marked disagreement. The degree of unanimity was striking, however. Certain qualities inherent in a gorgeous mineral, such as brilliance, sharp colors, damage-free crystals, and pleasing arrangement, seemed to appeal to everyone.

When the original list of 150 was refined to a "must" group of seventy-six, the judges frequently voted to retain some of the rarer species and to drop the more common minerals. In the Gallery these seventy-six are presented in an order calculated to delight the eye rather than merely to catalogue the final selections.

Not every judge helped select all minerals; some worked with as few as a half-dozen species. It was agreed that individual decisions of the judges would not be announced, but that consensus by a simple majority of the judges who worked with a particular species would result in the selection of the "finest example" for the Gallery.

The author accepts primary responsibility for decisions regarding which species of minerals would be represented in the Gallery. When such glamorous minerals as dioptase, axinite, and epidote are omitted, how is it possible to select two golds, two silvers, two rhodochrosites, and two siderites? When the judges split down the middle on some issues, the stalemate was resolved by including both pieces in the Gallery.

In some instances two forms of the same mineral are shown. This was done with siderite and rhodochrosite, because the types of each mineral varied to such a degree as to make them almost dissimilar.

CRITERIA FOR SELECTION

It was both interesting and revealing to hear the reasons judges gave for their selections. There was a definite pattern that was followed most of the time by nearly all judges. The following are the criteria most frequently used, but not necessarily in the order given:

1. Crystal perfection. Judges frowned on crystal damage, particularly to the termination faces. It was only when a particular specimen was of considerable interest that any injury to crystals was permitted. Occasionally, when it was virtually impossible to find a large specimen which was free of damage, the matrix with the least exhibited damage to the more important crystals was selected.

2. Matrix specimen. Other qualities being equal, preference was nearly always given to the crystals which occurred in clusters or which perched on another mineral.

3. Aesthetics. Judges were commonly attracted to a mineral where the arrangement of the components was especially pleasing.

4. Association. When the major mineral formed in combination with other minerals, preferably those which contrasted in color, brilliance, or shape, the specimen automatically registered extra points. Thus a black mineral, ordinarily unimpressive by itself, would take on new importance when it occurred with a white mineral such as quartz or calcite.

5. Color. The shade, hue, and intensity of a color were of great importance. Frequently the darker, but not duller, shades were preferred. For example, a dark-colored blue aquamarine crystal would receive more support than an equally well-formed but lighter-colored crystal.

6. Luster. Brightness gives sparkle to a mineral and nearly always resulted in more attention.

7. Size. Remarkably enough, size was not always a prime factor in selection. Many nominations were for very large specimens, but the judges generally preferred the smaller, perfect minerals, selecting larger specimens only if all other factors were equal.

By and large, the system used by the judges, though not in itself flawless, seems the best method yet devised.

It was the original plan to have as many collections as possible, both museum and private, represented in the book. Such an idea was doomed to an early disappointment. Classic minerals have certain qualities that tend to control their destinies: they are glamorous in appearance, they cause excitement among collectors, and they are valuable. Quite often a wealthy private collector gathers some of the unique minerals of our time, but his demise may cause the collection to be left with heirs who may have little or no interest in it. Consequently, many of the best private collections are eventually bequeathed to large museums. After years of this process, it becomes evident that major museum collections steadily get richer. Aggressive acquisition programs, substantial and knowledgeable staffs, sufficient storage and display areas, and reasonably adequate acquisition funds also foster outstanding collections. Thus a relatively few museums are more generously represented in the Gallery than others, but it is not the intent of this book to evaluate the institutions or their collections, but rather to select outstanding pieces from whatever sources. However, nowadays a growing number of private collectors have a substantial knowledge of mineralogy and possess the funds to compete with the more affluent museums for great new specimens when they become available. Some of their unique acquisitions are also illustrated in the Gallery.

Of the fine specimens nominated for the Gallery some could not be included because of the difficulties they present to the photographer. A number of rare and unusual species lack the qualities that would qualify them for adequate representation. All-white or all-black types, such as natrolite, tennantite, rutile, stephanite, and danburite, present special problems. The unbecoming phenomenon of flaws or fractures made the photographic presentation of the chosen axinite, alexandrite, barite, and linarite unfeasible. A few colored minerals—dioptase (dark green), scorodite (dark blue), and vanadinite (dark red)—lose much of their attractiveness when reproduced on color film in spite of the efforts of skilled photographers. Stringent control was exercised to show the crystals as they really are so that the reader would be able to identify the illustration with the specimen in the parent collection. For the sake of a reasonable uniformity in the Plates, some of the photographs were enlarged or reduced; the size of the actual mineral specimen is given in both centimeters and inches in the description on the facing page.

It would have been interesting to include minerals mined in Canada, Mozambique, Egypt, Ecuador, and Alaska, but selection was by quality, not locality. The Mining Location Map on pages 24 and 25 indicates the country or area where each mineral was mined; their broad geographic distribution is amazing.

A truly international atmosphere dominates the Gallery, with its illustrations of specimens mined at world-wide localities, owned and housed in museums and private collections in many countries, recommended or approved by hundreds of rock hounds, curators, collectors, and scientists, and photographed by skilled international photographers.

The author wishes to express particular gratitude to the core of judges, many of whom devoted much time in reviewing slides, photographs, and data. And a special thank-you to the curators who opened their doors, their records, and their knowledge for the undertaking. A warm acknowledgment also to the many photographers who showed genuine restraint and exercised great skill with a difficult assignment. And very special thanks to his wife, whose constant encouragement is deeply appreciated.

And, finally, the author will never forget the countless letters offering advice and encouragement. Among them was a note from fifteen-year-old Eric Rubenstein: "I became very enthused when I learned of your project, and I want so much to help you locate crystals for your book." In fact, Eric contributed several suggestions and thirty nominations. Possibly an encouraging comment by Rudy Fahl best summarized a major intent of the book: "Your idea of publishing a book on the world's finest minerals and crystals will bring out the beauty and wonder of God's creation."

I trust that the wishes of Eric and Rudy and all of the other contributors have been, at least in part, realized.

Peter Bancroft

THE BIRTH OF MINERALS

A museum visitor pausing before a cluster of crystals, marveling at its singular beauty, the vibrant hues, the perfection of the crystals, and its striking combination of minerals, may be totally unaware that in front of him exists a unique example of a particular species.

Well-formed museum-type display minerals and crystals are indeed rare. For each outstanding example, there are scores of lesser quality: some species of minerals do not (or at least have not) produced either large crystals or an abundance of them; many superb clusters are destroyed in mining; poor handling causes a major portion of all specimens to lose a part of their initial attractiveness. Those specimens which do survive man's carelessness and the capriciousness of nature become of great interest to the scientist and the layman alike. Let us look at the life cycle of three of the greatest specimens ever uncovered: each formed and grown differently from the others, each mined in a separate part of the world, each having survived a series of events any one of which could have caused its demise, and today each continuing its life in a setting quite apart from the others.

Picture, if you will, a small, black, shapeless lump of pure carbon located many miles deep in the earth millions of years ago. Centered in a gigantic molten mass of dense rock, it was subjected to enormous pressure and to temperatures of more than 1000 degrees centigrade. Hardly discernible changes began to take place in the anatomy of the carbon; the formation of a crystal had commenced. Deep under the African Continent, through the aeons of time, the aggregate continued to engulf the bit of carbon. Then weakness in the earth's crust permitted a vertical crack to develop; the superheated rock slowly pushed its way upward. Finally the mass lost its inertia and the bit of carbon came to rest a few hundred feet below the earth's surface, where the temperature was lower and the intense pressures gone.

Prior to and during the rough journey upward remarkable changes had been taking place in the carbon. Its color had changed from a dense black to a dazzling white. It had become transparent and very hard and was now the size of a man's fist, an immense crystal for its species. But, more important still, it had developed its own crystal form and, nearly complete, its new identity, clean and free from foreign particles or flaws. Other bits of carbon which started their growth in the same area had developed a murky appearance; some had cracked during the cooling process; most had remained small, a characteristic of crystallized carbon.

More years passed, during which the overburden was whisked away by the winds, until the crystal lay only thirty feet below the surface. Small sisters to the big crystal were found by prospectors who stood atop the "mother" mass of blue-colored rock. A mine was started and a shaft was sunk into the rock. Finally, in the year 1905, a miner pointed out the shiny crystal, still imbedded in the country rock, to the mine manager, Mr. F. Wells. With his pocketknife Wells carefully removed from its matrix the world's largest diamond crystal, weighing 3025 metric carats. Named the Cullinan in honor of the superintendent of the Premier Mine in which it had been found, it was sold to the Transvaal Government for $750,000 and was later cleaved into pieces from which 105 stones were cut. The largest section produced a unique stone, of great beauty, weighing 530 carats. Today, mounted in the King's Royal Scepter, it is displayed among the British crown jewels in London. Unfortunately, the original uncut crystal now exists only in photographs.

A second specimen, born in the back country of Brazil, started some millions of years ago as a glob of silicon dioxide in a quartz vein which coursed its way through a pegmatite structure in the earth. Temperatures were hot and the pressure was intense, but both were well below those encountered in the formation of the diamond crystal. Small crystals started to take shape, with each individual striving to complete its own form. Insufficient space caused many of the crystals to crowd into one another at the bases with only their tops or terminations standing free in the vein pocket. Some of these crystals were milky in color, while others were smoky.

Then a unique phenomenon occurred. New hot gases coursing through the vein brought not only additional silicon to the deposit but also small amounts of titanium, the coloring agent in rose quartz. This mineral-laden solution placed small crystals in little clusters about the bases of the original quartz spires. This event may have been the initial formation of rose quartz crystals in all of history.

But this masterpiece of nature still required a finishing touch. And so another breath of heated vapor entered the cavity, this time containing minute bits of aluminum, iron, and manganese. Mother Nature then "kissed" the large crystals lightly, leaving little groups of sparkling, brownish, eosphorite crystals about the termination faces. The masterpiece was complete in form, but many years would elapse before it had entirely cooled.

Its day of liberation came when Brazilian miners, working along the quartz vein, broke into the pocket which had protected the dainty crystals for so long. It was immediately recognized as a remarkable mineral sample. Carefully removed, wrapped, and sent to its new owner, H. Rudolf Becker in Idar-Oberstein, West Germany, this specimen helped convince an unbelieving mineral world that rose quartz could and does crystallize. Today it is considered the finest rose quartz matrix in the world; its portrait is Plate 52 in the Gallery of this book.

About six hundred miles west of Sydney, Australia, nearly a mile below the surface of the earth and some millions of years ago, there existed a large and very rich mass of lead and zinc minerals. Prominent in this mineral aggregate were the primary sulfides of galena and sphalerite with the mineralized mass surrounded in part by a great bed of limestone. Surface waters percolated downward into the ore body and then flushed back, bearing minerals in solution from the heavy rocks below. As the mineral-laden waters came to rest in the limestone formations nearer the surface, new oxide and carbonate minerals formed. One area in particular received an infusion of these lead-bearing waters, and as hundreds, perhaps thousands, of years passed, slender shafts of snow-white cerussite grew in the cavity. They formed in lattice-shaped or netlike bars, reticulated crystals. Because this pocket stayed hot and received new lead-filled waters for a longer period than did any other in the region, the bright new cerussite crystal group at its center was able to outgrow its neighbors in size and attractiveness. Miners working the Proprietary Block 14 Mine discovered and removed the matrix from its pocket and shipped it to the Australian Museum in Sydney, where today it is a featured display. This extraordinary specimen is pictured as Plate 16 in the Gallery.

Other fine minerals have had equally interesting beginnings, but these three illustrations demonstrate the unusual formative features of any unique specimen and the sometimes tortuous path it must follow before becoming secure as nature's legacy for future generations.

GIANTS AMONG THE EXPERTS

From the dawn of man's history to a few thousand years before Christ, new uses for rocks, minerals, and finally metals were discovered, usually by a process of trial and error or occasionally by luck. Progress was hampered by poorly kept records, little governmental interest, an incredible number of superstitions that seemed to touch nearly every known mineral, and the fact that the scientifically advanced were frequently considered to be misfits or, at best, curiosities.

Early Babylonians, Egyptians, and Asians were attracted to the crystals and mounds of colorful ores that they found scattered about the earth's surface. At first these minerals were gathered and used as household decorations. Serious mineral collecting possibly dates to these years. The more durable of the colorful stones (turquoise, amethyst, rock crystal, malachite, and lapis lazuli) were fashioned into jewelry. As time went on, the rarer and more desirable of the gems and metals became valued as barter as well as for their beauty.

Each culture seemed to develop its own techniques of working metals and fashioning stones. At the time of Christ substantial mining operations had commenced in a number of localities: the Egyptians were working gem and gold mines on the Upper Nile River, the Greeks were busy with their lead and zinc developments at Laurium, and Cornish miners were bringing tin to the surface. Supposedly magical minerals and gems had become popular as amulets and talismans because diamonds were thought to bring victory to the wearer; emeralds were believed to foreshow future events, jade to afford protection to the dead, lapis lazuli to be a cure for melancholy, loadstone (magnetite), placed beneath the pillow of a sleeping wife, to act as a touchstone of her virtue, a piece of malachite attached to an infant's cradle to ward off all evil spirits from the child, and a ruby inserted into the flesh to become a part of the owner's body and make him invulnerable to harm. In spite of omens and superstitions, a gradual change took place: brightly colored stones became attractive in themselves. Worn as a mark of distinction, they commanded attention and admiration for the wearer.

Possibly the first collector was Mithridates the Great, King of Pontus, who died in the year 63 B.C. He developed a superb collection that included gemstone crystals, precious minerals, and engraved stones.

In spite of the fact that the civilized world was now widely using bronze, gold, silver, and lead, no systematic method for the study of minerals had been developed. It is not known to whom the distinction of founding the science of mineralogy should be attributed; perhaps it belongs to the Greek philosopher Theophrastus, who (about 300 B.C.) wrote *On Stones,* the first known work to deal with mineral identification. Because some of his written records have survived, Theophrastus may be considered the first giant in the study of mineralogy. Pliny the Elder (A.D. 23–79) wrote a number of books dealing in part with mineral identification, ore classifications, and the superstition aspects of gemstones. These early works created some additional interest in the mining and use of minerals, but did little to sort out facts from a profound confusion of fantasy and superstition. Eventually, in 1546, the brilliant German, Georgius Agricola, wrote his book *De Re Metallica,* specifically considering mineral ore bodies, their identification and use. During the next century Thomas Nichols increased man's knowledge of gemstones when he wrote his *Lapidary, or History of Precious Stones.*

In the Middle Ages, the first recognized crystallographer, Johannes Kepler, used his knowledge of mathematics to demonstrate, through the growth of snow crystals and of artificial crystals, that all possess an internal crystalline structure as well as an external symmetry. There followed a succession of other important crystallographers, including Athanasius Kircher, Nicolaus Steno, and Romé de Lisle. Each made significant contributions to the field of mineralogy.

In 1784 René Just Haüy, Professor of the Natural History Museum in Paris, affirmed that crystals indeed do have an orderly internal structure; furthermore, he constructed a remarkable series of plates illustrating in the same drawing both the internal and the external crystal structures for today's study of crystals. René Haüy loved all minerals, and he frequently exchanged crystals with other collectors and museums, all the while developing a substantial personal collection, parts of which are now housed in the Natural History Museum in Paris.

Each of these giants opened doors for the first time to vast stores of information previously unknown. One cannot help but marvel at the skill of the metallurgist who nearly three thousand years earlier constructed Tutankhamen's solid-gold funeral mask and the wrought-iron headrest that was placed beneath the young king's neck. These wonders of ancient Egyptian craftsmanship represented metallurgical discoveries and a quality of artistry possibly unequaled today. But the tortuous steps of the discoveries that led to such work were unpretentious, infrequent, and, for the most part, unrecorded.

The emergence of complex studies of crystallography and mineralogy followed much the same path of discovery and utilization. Each phase was slow and frequently quite unspectacular, but the time was to arrive when a thorough knowledge of what minerals are, how they occur, and where they would likely be found would be a basic requirement for every degree-seeking geologist and mineralogist. Technology began to advance rapidly and reached a tremendous summit with the discovery of X-ray analysis as introduced by Max von Laue in 1912.

These early explorers who first unlocked mysteries of the earth-sciences have long since gone. Unfortunately, there were those among them whose discoveries and observations will never be known. But those of us who pause to marvel at the beauty of a fine crystal have a greater knowledge, a wider curiosity, and a more profound appreciation for what we are experiencing—because of the giants before us.

COLLECTORS AND COLLECTING

As the science of mineralogy developed and involved more specialists, universities, and museums, the art of collecting moved rapidly ahead. The first "dealers" became established institutions, with warehouses and display rooms, sales lists, catalogues, and directories of buyers, and periodic auctions. Collectors and dealers began to travel far and wide; the process of supplying fine minerals had become big business.

Although major private and public mineral collections were started in Europe during the eighteenth century, records are vague or lacking in detail.

Museums and schools of mines were the principal purchasers of fine minerals and the primary sources of technical data to encourage new mining techniques, which in turn produced new quantities of valuable mineral specimens.

A review of acquisition dates and other information on the labels of minerals in the older museums provides a wealth of interesting data. Some labels, written on paper that has long lost its resiliency, are tattered and faded beyond legibility. But others provide names of early collectors: L. M. Aylesford, London (1832); Dr. Eger, Copenhagen (1890); Richard Talling, London (1863); Count B. Lobkovic, Prague (1891); Carl Bisch, New York (1897); Émile Bertrand, Paris (1860); Monsieur Louis Taub, Paris (1888); Professor Waage, Oslo (1890); a Norwegian nobleman named Cappelen, Oslo (1895); V. M. Severgin, Moscow (1819); Abraham Werner, Freiberg (1809); and Graf Sternberg, Prague (1818). Unfortunately, not one of these collections survives intact today. Some individual extant specimens are quite ordinary, but this does not necessarily indicate that an entire collection was substandard. Frequently labels were lost in handling; in other cases, parts of a collection were damaged, misplaced, or exchanged. For various reasons, nearly all early original collections have been broken up and their records lost or destroyed.

The practice of conducting mineral auctions originated about the beginning of the nineteenth century. The first documented mineral auction was held in London in May 1812, by a Mr. Christie; in 1826 Mr. John Thomas held a sale in which he auctioned off a portion of the collection of Henry Heuland, one of the most intense and knowledgeable of the early dealers, who was traveling in search of minerals as far back as 1792. Occasionally such a sale would include fossils, seashells, and even art objects. Sales were well attended by the curators, collectors, and curious. Similar auctions are going on today in the "Great Rooms" of London firms that were doing business in the 1800s.

During the nineteenth century, collectors included members of the Danish, English, French, and Spanish royalty. Affluent Europeans pursued the elusive perfect mineral. This interest established price values and created an atmosphere that encouraged the salvage of fine crystals from the mines, and their continued preservation.

During these years most great private collections (some containing more than 40,000 specimens) reflected the skill, dedication, and technique of their owners. Nearly all emphasized various crystal forms, rare minerals, and, of course, beauty. Not a few included gem materials, both cut and rough. Some collectors housed their collections in specially crafted cabinets, some of the outstanding of which are those that were constructed by Henry Sjogren in 1892 and are displayed today in the north room of Stockholm's Royal Museum of Natural History with their minerals intact. Nearly all of these collectors printed their own labels, today treasured antiques in their own right. Many of these mineral connoisseurs bequeathed their collections to museums. The collections of William Neville (1870), Charles Hampton Turner (1818), and Henry Heuland (1835) are now in the British Museum (Natural History). The Academy of Natural Sciences in Philadelphia received those of Adam Seybert (1825) and William Vaux (1882). That of V. M. Severgin (1826) went to the Fersman Mineralogical Museum in Moscow, and that of A. F. Holden (1913) to Harvard University. The Smithsonian Institution inherited the collections of Mahlon Dickerson (1860), Frederick Canfield (1860), and Washington Roebling (1926). Henry Sjogren (1896) bequeathed his to the Royal Museum of Natural History, Stockholm. J. Pierpont Morgan (1913) and Clarence Bement (1910) both left theirs to the American Museum of Natural History.

At the turn of the century, the rush for good minerals was attracting hundreds of hobbyists of modest means. The schools of mines at Prague, Freiberg, Paris, Copenhagen, Leningrad, Bucharest, São Paulo, and Golden, Colorado, were sending out skilled young geologists, many already mineral lovers, to gather the best available material for themselves and their schools. A new group of advanced collectors was forming. At its head was Sir Arthur Russell of England who started collecting at the age of eight, in 1886, when he went underground into a Cornish tin mine in search of crystals. During his lifetime he collected 14,000 mineral specimens, many of them personally. He went into every working mine in England and as a result assembled one of the best collections of English material ever gathered. He discovered some new species and located others that had never before been found in England. Through outright purchase he added two superb additional collections: those which had belonged to Phillip Rashleigh (1728–1811) and to author John Ruskin (1819–1900). The quality of his efforts was publicly acknowledged through the bestowal of an honorary degree—Doctor of Science—at Oxford University. Upon his death in 1964 his collection passed on to the British Museum (Natural History) in London, where two cases of his minerals still are on public display at the entrance to the mineral hall. His witherite (personally collected) is presented as Plate 32 in the Gallery of this book.

A second great collector was Colonel Louis Vesignie, who gathered more than 40,000 specimens of minerals, gem crystals, meteorites, and cut stones. Upon his death in 1954 he left his collection to the Natural History Museum in Paris, where items from the collection are on display in a special room at the east end of the mineral hall. Of unusual interest are the gem crystals of tourmaline, topaz, and aquamarine, and the 100-carat cut alexandrite. There are also two very fine 25-carat diamond crystals.

One may see great private collections throughout the world, some of them containing unique specimens. Outstanding ones in the United States are those of George Bideaux, Tucson; Alfred Buranek, Salt Lake City; Rock Currier of Ardsley, and William Pinch of Rochester, New York; Philip Gregory and E. M. Gunnell of Denver; Richard Hauck, Bloomfield, New Jersey; F. N. Hickernell, Cavendish, Vermont; Thomas McKee, Paradise Valley, Arizona; Charles Key, St. Petersburg, Florida; and David Wilber, Reno, Nevada. Concentrated in California are the collections of George Holloway, Northridge; John Jago, San Francisco; Paul Patchick, Pebble Beach; William Sanborn, Newport Beach; John Sinkankas, San Diego; Edward Swoboda, Los Angeles; Roger Williams, Encino; and C. Douglas Woodhouse, Santa Barbara.

In Europe, there are the fine collections of Herman Bank and Gerhard Becker of Idar-Oberstein, and Godehard Schwethelm of Munich, in West Germany; Paul Fraenkel, Claude Guillemin, and Henri-Jean Schubnel in Paris; and Werner Burger of Zurich, Walter Hofer of Interlaken, Valentin Sicher of Gurtnellen, and H. Huguenin-Stadler of Altdorf, all Switzerland; Joaquin Folch Girona, Barcelona; Professor Th. Sahama, Helsinki; and Professor Heinz Meixner, Salzburg, Austria.

Other important collections are those of Albert Chapman, Sydney, Australia; Mette Sorensen, Narassak, Greenland; and Sydney Pieters, Windhoek, South-West Africa.

For the modern collector, the source of rare finds is often not the miner or producer but the individuals and companies dealing in minerals and gem material. There was a time when dealers employed local buyers stationed in the country where the material was produced, or at the mine itself in order to be first at the scene of a new discovery; nowadays, however, whole teams of buyers periodically flood an area. The Japanese, Germans, French, and Americans are particularly well organized. A buyer may have as many mine-shaft bosses as possible receptive to his offer to buy any outstanding specimens saved from the ore skips. Some companies own mines throughout the world, especially in Brazil. A very few dealers, knowing the location and quality of nearly every private collection, specialize in predicting (with uncanny accuracy) when one may be for sale.

There are a few wholesale dealers who deal in substantial quantities of specialized items and sell only to retailers, or who handle only material or minerals sized to one-inch or two-inch squares for study purposes, possibly in school laboratories.

There are hundreds of retailers in Europe and in the United States who welcome visitors to their stores or homes, and who occasionally travel with their specimens to mineral shows where they set up booths from which to vend their wares. Some dealers work with giant-size specimens, occasionally mounted in wood or metal for use as decorative showpieces, while others accept only mail orders.

Curators, collectors, and dealers alike explore new discoveries in a variety of publications devoted to gems and minerals. For many years the few magazines that existed were printed on shoestring budgets and had limited circulations. The development of color photography, offset printing, and the spectacular rise in the number of hobbyists have increased the number of magazines, improved their size and quality, and added a great many trade journals, society bulletins, and university and museum papers on the subject.

Many universities and museums publish booklets, some in color, which feature information about certain mineral species or which illustrate various specimens within the institutions' collections. Some museums print postcards depicting choice crystals in color, to be sold at the museum store or bookstall.

The curators, collectors, miners, photographers, cutters, metalsmiths, professors, research specialists, authors, editors, and the rock hounds who plan, scrape, and sweat —these are today's pioneers, the people with vision—these are the prospectors of our time.

HAZARDS

Conservationists all over the world are multiplying their efforts to keep the inland lakes and waterways clear and pure, to reduce exhaust emissions from the tail pipes of automobiles and the stacks of factories, and to conserve the dwindling numbers of the Indian rhinoceros, the Calfornia gray whale, and the quetzal of Central America.

Similar efforts are being exerted to preserve and safeguard a Ramses III Twentieth Dynasty carving, a T'ang Dynasty bronze, or an eighteenth-century painting by Sir Thomas Lawrence. Fortunes are being spent in the designing and construction of breathtaking art palaces where each masterpiece is maintained under strict controls of heat and humidity, and where the possibility of damage or loss by vermin, vandals, or thieves has been reduced to a minimum.

Equal treatment for the masterpieces of the crystal and mineral world simply does not exist. To begin with, the formation of perfect crystals is torturous and their preservation in nature capricious. Although Salzburg epidotes, Mesa Grande tourmalines, and Pikes Peak amazonstones may be formed originally as perfect crystals in pockets deep in pegmatite veins, earthquakes and percolating waters which freeze solid during the winter may cause a shearing action that seriously damages substantial numbers of crystals long before the miner opens the pocket. Or, since gem vugs are not spaced evenly along the pegmatite vein, explosives unknowingly placed too close to a valuable pocket may cause catastrophic damage to its contents. Small pockets of crystals, unnoticed by miners in the dim light, may be loaded aboard an ore car and dumped with the waste. Even when an undamaged crystal cleft has been located, safe removal is an arduous task. The trip out of the mine can result in additional damage. Each step in the process must be considered a hazard.

Disastrous fires have destroyed forever valuable minerals that had outlived the rigors of the mining and collecting processes. Other collections have been totally destroyed by the ravages of war. Poor handling or improper storage is responsible for a substantial amount of damage to good crystals. Over the years an inordinate number of brilliant yellow sulfur crystal groups, with most of the crystal faces in good condition, have come from Sicilian mines, yet of the hundreds studied for this book, only five were recommended for serious consideration; nearly every sulfur examined exhibited damage to the exterior of the crystals, damage which appeared to have occurred subsequent to mining.

Many minerals are lost each year because they are housed in flimsy or improperly constructed cases. Excessive heat from too many incandescent lamps wreaks havoc upon opals, crystals with water inclusions, and minerals with sensitive or unstable colors.

Some minerals should not be neighbors in the same case. This is particularly true of the sulfides and those minerals containing sulfur, since sulfur atoms will attempt to add themselves to, or remove elements from, other crystals. A crumbling chalcopyrite specimen may not be reacting to old age; the culprit could be a native sulfur crystal or a pyrite cluster in the next row of minerals. Recently a magnificent group of pyrargyrite crystals that had been nominated for this book collapsed into five or six pieces when it was picked up for inspection. The crystals had been naturally cemented together by a bond of pyrite that had decomposed over the years until its strength could no longer hold the specimen together.

A major social ill of our times—theft—has jeopardized the security of every superb mineral in the world. Mineral thieves today exercise all of the patience and skill demonstrated by the astute bank burglar. While museums and private collectors are rapidly installing ultrasonic and other protective devices, many installations are made after the fact. Tragic robberies removed the priceless emeralds from the American Museum of Natural History, the magnificent 133-carat white Colenso diamond crystal from the British Museum (Natural History), and a major portion of the remarkable mineral collection of Yale University. Private collections are being raided also. At least three collectors and one prominent European museum declined representation in this book fearing that publicity could direct undesirables to their collections. Many of the greatest crystal treasures have been lost forever because thieves immediately had them cut into stones usable for jewelry.

Many superb crystals and minerals are lost because they have great commercial value. Beautiful aquamarine, emerald, zoisite, and ruby crystals are diced into sizes and shapes appropriate for jewelry. Thus many of the world's best crystals are cut into fine stones because their value can thus be more easily redeemed. The Cullinan diamond, a 3025-carat crystal, by far the largest ever found, cut into more than one hundred stones, is now lost forever.

The largest model in the mineral collection of the British Museum (Natural History) is that of the Welcome Stranger gold nugget, which was found in February 1869 at Moliagul, Victoria, Australia. It weighed 2520 ounces and was valued at that time at £9534. Found by two prospectors in the roots of a tree where it had been disturbed by a passing cart, it was sold to a bank for its cash value and melted down. A stone obelisk marks the spot where it was discovered. Most probably a nugget of comparable quality will never again be found. Nearly all of the giant gold and platinum specimens displayed in the world's museums are only painted plaster casts.

Most devastating of all is the practice forbidding collecting on mine property. In gem mines crystals are immediately turned over to company representatives, but such is not the case with mines producing copper, lead, uranium, zinc, and other metals. There miners are not only discouraged from collecting; they may in some instances lose their jobs or even be arrested. Stopping work to collect or to "high-grade" the stopes is both costly and dangerous, but the losses of choice crystals under present systems must be incredible.

Some of the finest crystallized specimens of azurite and malachite remaining today came from the fabulous Copper Queen Mine at Bisbee, Arizona. During the years 1890 to 1910 employee collectors salvaged many bright blue and green clusters from the ore trains as they rumbled to the mill. Today the Phelps Dodge Corporation, owner of the Bisbee copper interests, authorizes some of its employees to collect in the mines mineral specimens which the company will offer for sale.

Until recently the copper and lead mine at Tiger, Arizona, employed a person whose job was to collect crystals in the mine and then to sell them in the mine's mineral store. Many beautiful crystals of dioptase, caledonite, linarite, cerussite, and wulfenite were saved and were sold to dealers and collectors. Unfortunately, this scheme came to a halt when the Collins shaft (the main workings of the mine) burned in 1966.

By contrast, a recent report revealed that workers in a mine at M'Passa in Zaire had discovered a giant pocket of very rare chalcocite crystals. An incredible fifteen tons of these crystals were estimated to lie within the vug. When orders were given to clean out the crystals and send them to the smelter, only ten specimens were saved by miners who were able to secrete them from the sharp-eyed shift boss.

Natural location contributes to the continuing shortage of minerals and crystals. Most ore bodies contain oxide or carbonate zones in their upper levels, while the heavier sulfides occupy the lower or bottom levels. Many of the world's most glamorous minerals frequently occur in the richest sections of the oxide zones—azurite, rhodochrosite, smithsonite, malachite, mimetite, calcite, and fluorite—in deposits extending upward to intersect with the surface as an outcrop. Such outcrops as those containing malachite or azurite (two of the brighter-colored minerals) frequently can be seen for several miles. Consequently, most of these deposits have been found and exploited, and the possibility of major oxide zones remaining undiscovered is remote indeed.

Many mines, however, do not have "rich" oxide zones, and thus produce few, if any, of the glamorous carbonate minerals. Worse, because most large copper and lead mines have been excavated through the oxide zone and are now working the lower or sulfide levels, fine oxide and carbonate minerals, already hard to find, may never again appear in quantity.

Although the demand for fine minerals is increasing, the supply of many species, unfortunately, is decreasing. Modern lovers of fine minerals must exercise every energy to conserve the classic specimens of our time, or future generations may have to direct their curiosities to a review of available photographs or to the study of plaster casts. While there are rocks of some sort nearly everywhere, extraordinary crystals, such as those illustrated in the Gallery, are truly in short supply.

A THIRD DIMENSION

The three-dimensional art of collecting minerals can be yours provided you have an ordinary curiosity, you are willing to devote a reasonable amount of time, and, most important, you have built into your emotional system at least a small portion of love of symmetry, color, and arrangement.

Superb minerals, crystals, and gems can stimulate the emotions as deeply as do the great works of music and of art. Although many rock and crystal lovers are at least partially unaware of the extent of their involvement, some have the ability to see familiar objects as fantasy in quite an ordinary piece of stone. Others see beauty in the features of a rock that may appear barren, drab, and uninteresting to someone else. Among the Japanese are those who, finding a particular pebble stimulating or comforting to the touch, keep it as a "feeling stone." These stones, carried in a pocket conveniently accessible to the hand, seldom have a distinct color and tend to be nondescript in appearance. Some command handsome prices.

More and more rocks, slabs, carvings, and stone objects are being included in the decor of homes, business offices, gardens, and the foyers of public buildings everywhere. Large clusters of crystals or masses of brightly colored ores are being combined with metals, plastics, and woods to form art objects for people who may never have owned a mineral specimen before.

Many collectors react strongly to the singular beauty of a well-crystallized specimen. They can see streams with moss-covered banks in the recesses and indentations, cliffs covered with pine trees along the prism faces, and mountain peaks in place of the terminations. These people are not "odd"; they have searched for and found true dimensional beauty in nature's handiwork.

Fortunes are spent each year for jewelry set with cut stones that are in reality the offspring of crystals and minerals. There are those who prefer a stone in its natural state of that of the cut and polished gemstone.

Throughout history, man has been captivated by eye-catching minerals. The concentration of vibrant colors and the perfection of crystal forms often create a singular beauty rivaled only by that of such masterpieces of nature as a butterfly's wing or a sunset. Today jewelers frequently enhance their glittering window displays by adding an appropriate crystal or two. Jewelry is fashioned by using natural crystals rather than cut stones in the mounting; even synthetic crystal clusters are mounted in gold.

Why are people so impressed by the beauty of crystals? If there is an answer, it must come from those involved. But one observation is certain—within the range of crystals, whether they are mined, studied, collected, or cut, there is something for nearly everyone. The rock hound can search out his own material in the mountains, valleys, and deserts. If he's fortunate, he can pack out as much as his back or automobile will hold. He can select the favorites for himself, discard the waste to the flower garden, and exchange the duplicates with his friends. If the rocks are gemlike, he can slab, preform, form, polish, or carve as his inclination and skills dictate. If you want to experience an extreme envy, look at an advanced collection in which each piece was found in the field by the owner, and absorb the atmosphere of adventure and achievement.

If he is to experience the full dimensional effect of his interest, each collector should first of all decide to do his own collecting, assess his circumstances, and go forward from there. Most outstanding collectors have certain qualities in common: they have learned a great deal about mineralogy and geology, have adequate financial resources, have time and opportunity for travel, are competitive and persistent by nature, are imaginative, have reasonable patience, and seem to have a substantial amount of good luck.

Many rock hounds specialize. Some stress crystal perfection; others acquire only minerals of a certain size. The apartment dweller can easily house an extensive collection of miniatures (each specimen limited to a size not exceeding 2″ × 2″), and the renter of a single bedroom can put a cabinet of three hundred thumbnail specimens ($1'' \times 1''$) under his bed. There are collectors who seem to derive every bit as much pleasure from peering through a microscope into the breathtaking small world of the micromount (minerals so small that individual crystals must be magnified to be easily seen) as those who do not live with such limitations.

Color is all-important to some hobbyists. Pastel colors of pink morganite, lavender amethyst, blue fluorite, or orange wulfenite, and the more vibrant, rich colors of dark-blue aquamarine or hemimorphite, jet-black cassiterite or tourmaline, or deep-green pyromorphite or dioptase both have their admirers. There are those who concentrate on rarity, with little concern for size or color. Still another group of mineral specialists resists any mineral not in combination or association with at least one other mineral in the same specimen. Other rapidly growing groups of enthusiasts limit their collections to specimens from a single locality or area, from one mine, or from one state or province.

Currently, nearly every rock that appears somewhat unusual becomes a salable item. Many department stores are doing a brisk business in minerals which advanced collectors would consider to be too large, imperfect, or of inferior quality. "Arty" pieces—those that may vaguely resemble a human face, a ship at sea, or a barn owl —make up collections of their own. And millions of highly polished, tumbled stones are being readied as premiums for cereal boxes.

In well-known mining regions or areas where there are many rock hounds, the odds are that the competition will have left little behind. Locales that are currently producing more material than can be absorbed by their own collectors are Mexico, Australia, Malagasy Republic, Mozambique, Switzerland, Canada, Brazil, and Chile. Areas such as the Pacific Islands, which are largely volcanic, produce a lesser variety of minerals.

Mineral dealers are an important source for collectors. They offer advice about how to build collections and keep on the lookout for requested specimens. Most dealers don't maintain personal collections and will frequently go out of their way to help the hobbyist to build his collection.

Advanced collectors, by and large, are busy people, but their intense interest in the hobby usually makes their experience available to the beginner.

The amateur who wants to become adept as a trader should have a reasonably good knowledge of market values, the availability of the particular minerals he wants, and what constitutes a fair, good, or excellent example of each species. He also needs to know the shortcomings and requirements of other collections—invaluable knowledge for an exchange.

Ardent collectors see that the crystals never bump each other or rub against a hard surface, and keep thick carpets before their cases as protection against dropping. Minerals must be kept dry, cool, and dust free. Good cases provide maximum display area, proper lighting, attractive presentation, and desirable security. The best light is usually incandescent, but this is hot and may require exhaust fans. Many exhibitors use pastel colors for backdrops and risers, while others use light gray, tan, or white. Since minerals are best not handled by others than the curator, locks on all cases are a good precaution. Valuable collections frequently need the added protection of ultrasonic alarm devices, windowless rooms, specially keyed locks, direct lines to the police station, alert neighbors, or safe-deposit boxes—any device designed to discourage the prowler.

Wisely and persistently accumulated, an expanding collection increases in value with each new acquisition. Poor minerals will always be cheap; good minerals maintain their value, with crystals in the "superb" class increasing their worth at an astonishing rate. It is safe to say that choice minerals have doubled in value during the past five to ten years; few other hobbyists work with objects the values of which escalate so dramatically. Before you sell that collection that has lain dormant in the basement for the past decade, become knowledgeable about current price trends. You may decide to keep your collection for at least another ten years.

The wonderful friends the collector makes through his hobby may lead him to collecting areas he never knew existed, and can help to locate other collectors, dealers, and cutters. Best of all, he finds new sources of pleasure—new places to see, new activities to enjoy, and new friends to rejoice at his successes. Those who work at their collections with persistence and vigor realize the unique personal thrills of full involvement, and, upon occasion, may become the proud possessors of treasures that will take their place among the world's finest minerals and crystals.

MINING LOCATIONS

WASHINGTON

NEW HAMPSHIRE

COLORADO

NEW YORK

CALIFORNIA

ARIZONA

NORTH CAROLINA

BAJA CALIFORNIA

MEXICO

COLOMBIA

BOLIVIA

BRAZIL

CHILE

SCALE ON EQUATOR

| 0 | 1000 | 2000 | 3000 MILES |

0   1000   2000   3000   4000   KILOMETERS

MERCATOR PROJECTION

HML

Goode Base Map Series, Department of Geography, the
University of Chicago. Copyright by the University of Chicago.

THE GALLERY

Gold Crystals
Aquamarine
Mimetite
Apatite
Anglesite
Wulfenite
Millerite
Benitoite
Silver Crystals
Phosphophyllite
Pyrargyrite
Smithsonite
Fluorite
Cuprite
Hauerite
Skutterudite
Boleite
Thorianite
Malachite (Pseudomorph)
Cerussite
Uvarovite
Azurite
Euclase
Galena
Cinnabar
Siderite
Ruby
Smaltite
Golden Topaz
Aquamarine Matrix
Orthoclase
Hiddenite
Malachite (Pseudomorph after
Azurite)
Anatase
Rhodochrosite (Pseudomorph
after Calcite)
Witherite
Spangolite
Stibnite

Autunite
Phosgenite
Chalcocite
Morganite
Smoky Quartz
Diamond
Smithsonite (Reniform)
Wolframite
Realgar
Magnetite
Native Silver
Brookite
Sulfur
Tanzanite
Acanthite
Amazonstone (Amazonite)
Calcite
Rose Quartz
Legrandite
Perovskite
Anhydrite
Cassiterite
Crocoite
Proustite
Ludlockite
Blue Topaz
Sperrylite
Amethyst
Stolzite
Native Gold
Grossular
Emerald
Rhodochrosite
Kunzite
Erythrite
Siderite (Pseudomorph after
Fluorite)
Brazilianite
Rubellite (Red
Tourmaline)

The Plates

GOLD CRYSTALS

Collection: British Museum (Natural History)
Curator: Peter Embrey
Size: 12.7 cm × 6.1 cm; 5″ × 2.4″

Gold has been an important factor in changing the destiny of man. It has challenged his imagination and has caused his demise by countless thousands. Early in California's fabled Gold Rush, Horace Greeley wrote in his newspaper the *Tribune,* "We are on the brink of an Age of Gold." Today the mining of gold in low-grade ore bodies or in stream beds has lost much of its glamour, but nearly every visitor to a mineral collection wants to know where the gold specimens are, if he hasn't already found them. Many of the golds are pieces of rock, some of it snow-white quartz, in which are imbedded flakes, strings, or whole masses of gold. Crystals are unusual; well-defined, large crystals are most rare. Some crystals grow into graceful feather-shaped fronds of little shiny plates. Occasionally a well-defined single crystal of good size is seen, but when the judges for this book were asked, "Where is the best example of crystallized gold?", many of them responded, "In the British Museum."

This specimen received its name, "Latrobe," from the facts involving its discovery. On May 1, 1835, Charles Joseph Latrobe, Governor of the State of Victoria in the Commonwealth of Australia, was visiting the McIver Mount gold mine. Word came to the office that an unusual and large nugget had been found. It was shown to the governor and was named the Latrobe Gold Nugget in his honor. What no one seemed to realize was that while this nugget was small as nuggets go (weight 23 ounces Troy—717 grams), it was and still is the largest and best-formed crystallized gold known. Some of its cubes are more than half an inch in size, and the whole mass is made of gold cubes. The richness of color is due to the existence of a small percentage of copper in its composition. This gold was sold to the British Museum (Natural History) in 1856; for security reasons a cast was made for the display case, while the specimen itself resides in a safe deep inside the museum, where it is unseen by the public.

Other fine gold crystal specimens are in the collections of the University of Witwatersrand, Johannesburg, South Africa, and the Wells Fargo Bank Museum, San Francisco.

Nominated by Claude Guillemin, Paris
Photographed by Peter Green and Frank Greenaway, London

AQUAMARINE

Collection: The Smithsonian Institution
Curator: Paul Desautels
Size: 24 cm × 8.9 cm; 9.5″ × 3.5″

Aquamarine is the blue or blue-green member of the beryl family. It has the necessary characteristics of a gemstone, including better-than-average hardness, desirable brilliance, sufficient rarity, and, of considerable importance, pleasing colors. Aquamarine is a beryllium aluminum silicate. Its crystals form in long, hexagonal-shaped prisms, most frequently with flat or nearly flat terminations. One of the largest gem-quality aquamarines ever found weighed 243 pounds and came from Morambaya, Minas Gerais, Brazil. "Transparent from end to end," it was mined in the 1920s and sold originally for $25,000. Other fine aquamarine crystals have been reported from the island of Elba, Italy; the Mourne Mountains, County Down, Ireland; the Adun-chilon Mountains, Nerchinsk, Transbaikalia; Miask, the Ural Mountains; and Mursinsk, Ekaterinburg, all U. S. S. R.; the Habachtal, Salzburg, Austria; Santa Rita de Arassuahy and Teofilo Otoni, both Minas Gerais, Brazil; Royalston, Worcester County, Massachusetts; Mount Antero, Chaffee County, Colorado; and Rincon, San Diego County, California.

This specimen was obtained by the Smithsonian Institution in 1962 from the Parser Mineral Corporation of Connecticut. It was found near Teofilo Otoni. While there exist a number of larger choice aquamarine crystals, this specimen was selected for its clarity, rich color, and crystal perfection. The specimen number in the Smithsonian Collection is 115228.

Other outstanding aquamarines are in the collections of the Fersman Mineralogical Museum, Moscow; Herman Bank, Idar-Oberstein, West Germany; Petronio Miglio, Teofilo Otoni, Brazil; Harvard University; the American Museum of Natural History; the School of Mines, Paris; the Museum of Natural Science, Milan; the Feire de Andrade Museum, Lourenço Marques, Mozambique; and the Natural History Museum, Santa Barbara, California.

Nominated by Robert Swader, Arlington, Virginia
Photographed by Earl Lewis, Los Angeles

MIMETITE

Collection: Gerhard Becker, Idar-Oberstein, West Germany
Size: 7 cm × 4.5 cm; 2.8″ × 1.8″

Mimetite is chemically formed of lead and arsenic and contains a small amount of chlorine. It most frequently occurs in the ore bodies of lead mines, and as such is a minor ore of lead. Usually mimetite forms in brown or yellowish masses that resemble iron rust. Sometimes the crystals form into rounded aggregates of mammillary-shaped crusts. Fine translucent crystals have been found at Santa Eulalia, Mexico; Mammoth, Arizona; Transbaikalia, U. S. S. R.; and Johanngeorgenstadt, Saxony, East Germany. Transparent crystals were virtually unknown until a series of small pockets of gem-clear mimetite crystals were found in the Tsumeb, South-West Africa, lead mine. This mine has produced outstanding examples of crystallized copper, lead, and iron minerals since it first opened in 1851.

This beautiful group of yellow mimetite crystals has been judged the best of its kind in existence. The largest crystal is 2.3 cm, nearly one inch long. It was found at Tsumeb in 1971.

Other fine mimetites are in the collections of the Smithsonian Institution; the School of Mines, Freiberg, East Germany; the Natural History Museum, Vienna; the School of Mines, Madrid; the Faculty of Sciences, Paris; the British Museum (Natural History) and the Geological Museum, London; and Sydney Pieters, Windhoek, South-West Africa.

Nominated by Edward Swoboda, Los Angeles
Photographed by Karl Hartmann, Sobernheim, West Germany

APATITE

Collection: Joaquin Folch Girona, Barcelona, Spain
Size: 11.3 cm × 10.5 cm; 4.4″ × 4.1″

Apatite commonly occurs throughout the world either as microscopic crystals or as very large mineral bodies. Crystals up to one inch in size are not uncommon; some Canadian crystals have reportedly weighed more than one quarter of a ton. Fine, transparent crystals are unusual and are highly prized by the collector. Apatite is of average hardness and brilliance, but its many hues (ranging from green to violet to pink to white and yellow) are some of the most pleasant to be seen in any mineral. Many apatites are fluorescent, and not a few are phosphorescent. It is essentially a mineral composed of the elements calcium, fluorine, and chlorine. Its crystals are hexagonal and prismatic in shape. Werner, in 1788, named the mineral "apatite," which in Greek means "deceive"; earlier mineralogists had thought that apatites were in reality beryl, quartz, fluorite, or diopside. Fine apatites have been found in the Swiss alpine clefts at the Rhonegletscher, at Reuss Gorge near Intschi, and at Val Cristallina. Other choice crystals have been found at Schlaggenwald, Bohemia, Czechoslovakia; Biella, Piedmont, Italy; Cerro de Mercado, Durango, Mexico; the Siglo Vente mine at Catavi, Bolivia; and Mount Apatite, Auburn, Maine, where the deepest-colored purple apatites are found.

This specimen was discovered in the fabulous Minas do Panasqueira at Fundão, Portugal, in 1966. The mines of this region in the past few years have produced thousands of glamorous mineral specimens of arsenopyrite, wolframite, quartz, apatite, pyrite, and other minerals, usually in most interesting association. There are larger apatite specimens of fine quality in existence, but for all-around beauty and for the amazing combination of well-crystallized minerals, this specimen received the nomination. It was obtained by Joaquin Folch Girona from a local dealer in Fundão in 1967. In the specimen, the black crystal is wolframite, the white crystal is quartz, the yellowish coating on the quartz crystal is cookite, and the hexagonal purple crystal is the apatite.

Other fine apatites are in the collections of Godehard Schwethelm, Munich; the Natural History Museum, Bonn; the School of Mines, Freiberg, East Germany; the British Museum (Natural History); Harvard University; the Smithsonian Institution; the Natural History Museum, Vienna; the National Museum, Prague; and the Fersman Mineralogical Museum, Moscow.

Nominated by Stephen Smale, Berkeley, California
Photographed by Francisco Bedmar, Barcelona, Spain

34

ANGLESITE

Collection: British Museum (Natural History)
Curator: Peter Embrey
Size: 9.5 cm × 8.3 cm; 3.75″ × 3.3″

Anglesite is an important ore of lead. It is usually a very brilliant mineral and occurs in white, gray, green, blue, and yellow colors. It is brittle, soft, and quite heavy. Anglesite crystals are generally prismatic in form and occur by the oxidation of galena in the oxidation zones of lead mines. Associated minerals are pyromorphite, linarite, caledonite, wulfenite, mimetite, and sulfur. Anglesite was first found and was named after the locality of Pary's mine on the island of Anglesey, Wales. It has also been found in fine crystals at Sidi-Amor-ben-Salen, Tunisia; Nerchinsk, Siberia, U. S. S. R.; Littfeld, Westphalia, West Germany; Bleiberg, Carinthia, Austria; Leadhills, Dumfries, Scotland; Huelgoat, Brittany, France; Monte Poni, Sardinia, Italy; Broken Hill, New South Wales, Australia; Zeehan, Tasmania, Australia; Sierre de los Lamentos, Chihuahua, Mexico; the Wheatley mine, Phoenixville, Chester County, Pennsylvania; Coeur d'Alene, Shoshone County, Idaho; and Castle Dome, Yuma County, Arizona.

This spectacular specimen was found in the 1850s at Matlock, Derbyshire, England. In 1862 Dr. Cantrell of Hirksworth, Derbyshire, exchanged the piece with the British Museum (Natural History). It has very large, well-formed, and quite yellow crystals. The largest crystal measures 5.1 cm long (2.1″), and its number in the collection is 34732.

Other choice anglesites are found in the collections of the School of Mines, Paris; the University Museum, Liège, Belgium; and the School of Mines, Madrid.

Nominated by Lloyd Tate, San Marcos, Texas
Photographed by Peter Green and Frank Greenaway

WULFENITE

Collection: Harvard University
Curator: Clifford Frondel
Size: 10.2 cm × 6.4 cm; 4″ × 2.5″

Fine wulfenite specimens display some of the most exotic colors to be found in the mineral world. Wulfenite's colors and their various hues range from honey-yellow, through olive-green, to orange and fire-engine red. While crystals are relatively soft, many display a luster and brilliance producing a rich visual effect. Obviously, good-quality, damage-free crystal clusters are in great demand for mineral collections. Wulfenite is sought as an ore of molybdenum and lead. Fine crystals of wulfenite have been found at Sidi Rouman, Tebessa, Algeria; Mindouli, Congo; Jebel Mahser, Morocco; Pribram, Bohemia, Czechoslovakia; the Christmas Gift Mine, Chillagoe, Queensland, and Broken Hill, New South Wales, Australia; Sierra de los Lamentos, Chihuahua, Mexico; the Mammoth Mine, Santa Catalina Mountains, Pinal County, Arizona; and areas near Tombstone, Cochise County, Arizona. Wulfenite is named after F. X. Wulfen, S.J. (1728–1805), a prominent Austrian mineralogist of his time.

This wulfenite was selected from hundreds of choice specimens because of the splendid color, the size of the crystal, and the fact of its being a matrix (limonite). It was found in the 1920s in the Red Cloud Mine located in the Trigo Mountains of Yuma County, Arizona. The Red Cloud Mine has produced some of the most vivid red and orange-colored lead minerals in existence; good crystals are still occasionally discovered in its deep and lonely recesses. This specimen was bought as a part of Harvard's Burrage Collection and is numbered 98351.

Other fine wulfenites are in the collections of Thomas McKee, Paradise Valley, Arizona; George Bideaux, Tucson, Arizona; the Museum of Central Africa, Tervuren, Belgium (a magnificent, very large orange crystal); the School of Mines, the Faculty of Sciences, and the Natural History Museum, all of Paris; the British Museum (Natural History); the Geological Museum, Pretoria, South Africa; and the Smithsonian Institution.

Nominated by Jack Winters, Boston, Massachusetts
Photographed by Earl Lewis

MILLERITE

Collection: The Smithsonian Institution
Curator: Paul Desautels
Size: 12.7 cm × 15.3 cm; 5″ × 6.1″

Millerite is an ore of nickel and rarely forms in delicate radiating clusters of brass-yellow crystals. These slender crystals grow in cavities with other nickel and iron minerals. Sometimes millerite intergrows into a hairlike mass which is dull and shabby when compared to the brilliant capillary crystals that have grown in calcite or limonite vugs. Millerite is a low-temperature mineral. Good crystals have been found at Keokuk, Iowa; St. Louis, Missouri; Johanngeorgenstadt, Saxony, East Germany; and Orford Township, Quebec, Canada. It was named for the mineralogist who first identified the mineral, Mr. H. W. Miller (1801–1880).

This remarkable specimen illustrates a group of millerite crystals radiating in a pocket of the iron mineral hematite. It was found in the Sterling mine at Antwerp, New York. The very fine Smithsonian mineral collection also contains a smaller high-quality millerite, but the judges ruled the millerite illustrated here to be the superior specimen. It came to the Smithsonian Institution in October 1927 as a part of the original Frederick A. Canfield Collection. Its collection number is C24.

Other good millerite specimens are in the collections of the School of Mines, Freiberg, East Germany; the National Museum, Prague; and Douglas Reif, Kalona, Iowa.

Nominated by John Jago, San Francisco
Photographed by Earl Lewis

BENITOITE

Collection: Josephine Scripps, San Luis Rey, California
Size: 21.6 cm × 12.7 cm; 8.5" × 5"

Benitoite was first found in 1907 in a lonely mountain range near Coalinga, California, and was thought to be sapphire; only isolated mercury and chromium mines were being worked at that time in the area. The benitoite crystals were bright and gemmy and had the rich cornflower-blue color of sapphire. It was not until sometime later that the crystals were determined to be too soft to be sapphire, and, therefore, that a beautiful new gemstone had been born. It was named "benitoite" since the mine was located on the San Benito River. Benitoite, being softer than most gemstones, proved a disappointment commercially because of its poor wearing quality. The supply was also quite limited, but the crisp brilliance and lovely blue color of the gem made it very desirable for mineral and gem collections. Stones were usually cut in "step" or "brilliant" forms. The benitoite crystals occur in snow-white natrolite veins running through the green serpentine country rock. The crystals are usually recovered from the carbonate matrix by leaching them out with acid. Most benitoites are smaller than one inch and tend to feather, so that good-sized flawless stones are very unusual. The largest cut benitoite of good quality weighs only 6.5 carats and is in the collection of the Smithsonian Institution. Benitoite associates with neptunite, chalcocite, chrysocolla, actinolite, albite, calcite, joaquinite, aragonite, and psilomelane. The benitoite mine is located about nine miles southeast of the New Idria quicksilver mine, San Benito County, California. It is not found in good quality or quantity anywhere else in the world.

This specimen has been judged as the finest known benitoite matrix because of the size and quality of the crystals, the pleasing association of the white natrolite, and the size of the matrix. It was mined in 1956. It was acquired by Miss Scripps after an offer through the mails, and she bought it sight unseen.

Other fine benitoite specimens are in the collections of Edward Swoboda, Los Angeles; and the American Museum of Natural History.

Nominated by Glen Frost, La Jolla, California
Photographed by Earl Lewis

SILVER CRYSTALS

Collection: The Mining Museum, Kongsberg, Norway
Size: Large group: 11 cm × 9 cm; 4.4″ × 3.5″
    Small twin crystal: 6.5 cm × 4.9 cm; 2.2″ × 1.9″

Silver crystals are uncommon; crystals of .3″ are most unusual. The crystals of the large group pictured here measure nearly .5″, and there are fifteen of them on the specimen. Many are shaped as well-formed cubes. The smaller specimen is the largest known silver crystal and is unique. It is a fine example of a twin crystal; the "twin" is determined by the small "v" at the top or termination. A small, native silver wire adheres on the lower left side of the crystal. Many judges of choice minerals consider this little crystal to be the single best example of silver in the world.

These specimens are a part of the Mining Museum's fabulous collection of silvers. Nowhere else may one see such an array of silver wires and crystals. The ride out to Kongsberg from Oslo to see the silver specimens in this museum should be a "must" for the mineralogist and lover of natural art. Cabinets of shiny wires extend from one end of the large silver collection room to the other. Other silvers are placed under glass cases atop ancient ore cars that have long since rumbled on their last trips through the dim tunnels of the Kongsberg mines.

These specimens were mined in Guds Hjelp i Nød Mine (God's Help in Distress Mine) in 1934. They were found deep in the mine some three hundred meters below sea level. This mine closed in 1956; while it is always possible for a mine to reopen, Kongsberg mining experts are not optimistic about the prospect. It well could be that really choice silver wires may never again be found in abundance. Thus, existing silvers will become more rare with the passage of time, and outstanding specimens will create more attention—particularly those in the Mining Museum of Kongsberg.

Nominated by C. Douglas Woodhouse, Santa Barbara, California
Photographed by Teigens Fotoatelier, Oslo

PHOSPHOPHYLLITE

Collection: Edward Swoboda, Los Angeles
Size: 7.6 cm $\times$ 5 cm; 3″ $\times$ 2″

One of the rarest of all minerals is the beautiful blue-green zinc, iron, and manganese phosphate called phosphophyllite. It is a remarkable mineral because of its pleasing color, brilliance, and clarity, but it is too soft to cut. However, its vibrant, nearly fluorescent blue-to-green color and its uncommon occurrence have combined to make this mineral one of the most desired of all species. It was originally found in 1913 in small, light-colored crystals at Hagendorf, Oberpfalz, Bavaria. It occurred as a secondary mineral in a pegmatite associated with sphalerite, apatite, vivianite, and a number of quite rare minerals. Phosphophyllite attracted little attention until a series of seams containing the mineral were found in solid iron pyrite at a depth of 2000 feet in the largest silver and tin mine at Potosi, Bolivia. Potosi is an old Bolivian mining camp which rests at an altitude of nearly 15,000 feet in the Andes. It was from the Cerro de Potosi centuries ago that the Spaniards extracted enough silver to finance one of their armadas, which proved to be unsuccessful against the British fleet. A very few fine-colored and well-formed crystals of phosphophyllite were discovered about 1950 and were so prized that Bolivian miners were threatened with arrest if they were caught with the crystals. Most crystals were between a quarter and a half inch in size.

This extraordinary crystal is nearly twice as large as the next largest. It possesses extremely rich color and is transparent through much of the crystal. It was collected by a Bolivian named Aurilio Bustos and was obtained by Edward Swoboda in September 1971.

Other fine phosphophyllite crystals are in the collections of the American Museum of Natural History; Philip Gregory, Denver, Colorado; the Smithsonian Institution; the School of Mines, Paris; and Peter Bancroft, Ramona, California.

Nominated by Robert Ramsey, San Diego, California
Photographed by Earl Lewis

PYRARGYRITE

Collection: British Museum (Natural History)
Curator: Peter Embrey
Size: 12.2 cm × 7.8 cm; 4.8″ × 3.1″

These black crystals of pyrargyrite have grown in a bed of amethyst crystals; this pairing provides one of the more beautiful combinations seen in the mineral kingdom. Pyrargyrite, a primary ore of silver, is formed by warm ascending solutions of silver being deposited in the upper levels of silver mines. It is commonly associated with proustite, galena, tetrahedrite, sphalerite, calcite, and quartz. Pyrargyrite is an uncommon mineral; good crystals are rare indeed. Pyrargyrite possesses a deep-red color when formed but frequently tarnishes to a solid-black color when exposed to sunlight for a long period of time. Fine pyrargyrites have been found at Durango, Mexico; Guadalajara, Hiendelaencina, Spain; Andreasberg, Harz Mountains, East Germany; Příbram, Bohemia, Czechoslovakia; Colquechaca, Bolivia; Chanarcillo, Atacama, Chile; Virginia City, Nevada; and Cobalt, Ontario, Canada.

This black-and-lavender specimen was found about 1870 at the century-old Valencia Silver Mine near Guanajuato, Mexico. It was sold to the British Museum (Natural History) by Nathaniel Davidson, Esq., in 1875. The largest pyrargyrite crystal on this specimen measures 2.61 cm (1″) long. Six other crystals are more than one-half inch long. The specimen is numbered BM 48539.

Other fine pyrargyrites are shown in the collections of Harvard University; the American Museum of Natural History; the Smithsonian Institution; the Fersman Mineralogical Museum, Moscow; the School of Mines, Freiberg, East Germany; the National Museum, Prague; the School of Mines, Paris; and George Holloway, Northridge, California.

Nominated by Charles Key, St. Petersburg, Florida
Photographed by Peter Green and Frank Greenaway

SMITHSONITE

Collection: David Wilber, Reno, Nevada
Size: 10.7 cm × 10.6 cm; 4.2″ × 4.1″

This magnificent smithsonite matrix disputes the statements of mineral book authors who, prior to 1960, wrote that smithsonite was essentially a mineral found only in very small crystals. During the last decade Tsumeb, South-West Africa, produced in modest quantities clusters of small smithsonite crystals in colors of white, green, pink, lavender, and yellow. Pink crystals were more prevalent than the other colors, and crystals of one inch were considered to be extremely large. Only a few yellow crystals were found, and inevitably these were of small size.

This specimen was found at Abenab (near Tsumeb), South-West Africa, in 1969. The largest crystal measures 5.6 cm × 3.8 cm (2.2″ × 1.5″). This matrix was selected because of its giant crystals, exceptional color, crystal perfection, and pleasing arrangement of the minerals on the specimen.

Other fine smithsonites are in the collections of the Faculty of Sciences and the School of Mines, both in Paris; the British Museum (Natural History); Harvard University; the Smithsonian Institution; and the National Museum, Prague.

Nominated by Robert Ramsey, San Diego, California
Photographed by Earl Lewis

FLUORITE

Collection: Natural History Museum, Bern, Switzerland
Curator: H. A. Stalder
Size: 14.2 cm × 8.7 cm; 5.6″ × 3.5″

Beautiful crystals of the calcium-fluoride mineral fluorite are found in many localities throughout the world. The crystals form in the shape of cubes or octahedrons and appear in a wide range of colors, including sky-blue, blue-green, light or dark green, yellow, brown, violet, white, colorless, gray, black, and, rarely, pink-to-red. The crystals are frequently bright, occur in wonderful groups, and sometimes associate with quartz, calcite, barite, galena, dolomite, and anhydrite. Some crystals possess a distribution of colors which occur in zones parallel to the crystal faces. These specimens when of good quality are highly prized. Many fluorites fluoresce and some phosphoresce. Fluorite is used as an essential ingredient of hydrofluoric acid, as a flux in the manufacture of steel, and as an element in the making of glass. The Chinese and Japanese have carved the blue and green varieties into exotic forms which grace many a display in museums and in private homes. Outstanding fluorite crystals have been found at Weardale, Durham, England (water-clear purple and green); Cleator Moor, Cumberland, England (very large crystals of yellow and lavender); Freiberg, East Germany (rich blue); Schlaggenwald, Bohemia, Czechoslovakia (associated with chalcopyrite and apatite); Monte Realejo, San Luis Potosi, Mexico (clear light green); Rosiclare, Hardin County, Illinois (large yellow, orange, and purple); Muscalonge Lake, Jefferson County, New York (large green cubes); Clay Center, Ottawa County, Ohio (water-clear brown cubes); Castle Dome, Yuma County, Arizona (lavender octahedrons); and Madoc, Hastings County, Ontario, Canada (in crystals of optical quality).

This specimen was selected from hundreds of lush crystals exhibiting a multitude of fairyland colors. Pink fluorite is usually most prized of all the colors, because of its dainty and pert crystals and also because of its rarity. This specimen is an outstanding example of the pink variety. It was found during the construction of the Druckschacht power plant at Göschenen, Switzerland, in 1958. It occurred in solid granite (as do most pink fluorites), and great care was exerted to avoid damaging the crystals during their removal; also in 1958 it was presented to the Bern Natural History Museum by Mr. Kaspar Nell of Göschenen.

Other fine pink fluorites are in the collections of E. M. Gunnell, Denver, Colorado; the Natural History Museum, Vienna; Edward Swoboda, Los Angeles; the Museum of Natural History, Grenoble; the Natural History Museum, Paris; the British Museum (Natural History); and the Humboldt University, Berlin.

Nominated by Peter Indergand, Göschenen, Switzerland
Photographed by Karl Buri, Bern, Switzerland

CUPRITE

Collection: British Museum (Natural History)
Curator: Peter Embrey
Size: 8.8 cm × 6 cm; 3.5″ × 2.7″

Cuprite is a red copper mineral which forms in cubic or octahedral (eight-sided) crystals. It is fairly soft, brittle, and occasionally transparent. While cuprite is a common mineral, it seldom occurs in crystals more than one-half inch in size. It easily pseudomorphs (retains its crystal shape but changes chemically to another mineral) to malachite and native copper. It frequently coats native copper and ancient copper and bronze artifacts with small crystals. "Cuprite" was derived from the word "cuprum," meaning copper. Good crystals have been found at Redruth, Cornwall; Chessy, Lyons, France; Szaszka, Banat, Hungary; Bogoslovsk, U. S. S. R.; Rheinbreitbach, Siegen, Westphalia, West Germany; Broken Hill, New South Wales, Australia; Queenstown, Tasmania, Australia; Shaba, Zaire; Tsumeb, South-West Africa; Arakawa, Japan; Corocoro, La Paz, Bolivia; and Bisbee, Arizona.

This beautiful specimen was purchased in 1873 by the British Museum (Natural History) from Mr. R. Talling. It was found in the Phoenix mine near Liskeard, Cornwall, in 1868. The size of the largest crystal is 3.1 cm (1.2″) long. The specimen's number is 46255.

Other fine cuprites are in the collections of the Bank of Bisbee in Bisbee; Thomas McKee, Paradise Valley, Arizona; the University of Copenhagen; the Fersman Mineralogical Museum, Moscow; the Museum of Central Africa, Tervuren, Belgium; the School of Mines, Paris; and the Sengier-Cousin Museum at Jadotville, Shaba, Zaire.

Nominated by George Botham, London
Photographed by Peter Green and Frank Greenaway

HAUERITE   Size: 7.5 cm × 7.5 cm; 3″ × 3″ (upper right)
SKUTTERUDITE   Size: 9.5 cm × 6.5 cm; 3.7″ × 2.4″ (upper left)
BOLEITE   Size: 1.9 cm × 1.9 cm; .75″ × .75″ (center right)
THORIANITE   Size: 9 cm × 9 cm; 3.4″ × 3.4″ (lower left)
MALACHITE   Size 4.5 cm × 4.5 cm; 1.75″ × 1.75″ (lower right)
(Pseudomorph)

> Collection: School of Mines, Paris
> Curator: Claude Guillemin

The School of Mines Mineralogical Museum in Paris is very rich in fine minerals. Its superb crystal collection reflects the wisdom and energy of its director, Claude Guillemin. Shown here are five specimens, each unique in crystal form, perfection, and size. Possibly no other museum is capable of producing five such magnificent crystals.

HAUERITE   This specimen was found in the Destricella mine at Raddusa, Sicily, in 1892. It was presented to the museum in 1893 by a Mr. Baraffael, the chief engineer for the mine. Hauerite, an extremely rare mineral, is primarily manganese; it usually occurs with gypsum and sulfur. It has also been found at Collingwood, New Zealand. The collection number is 603.

SKUTTERUDITE   The specimen contains cobalt, arsenic, and nickel. This uncommon mineral seldom occurs in well-formed crystals more than one inch in size. It was named after the locality, Skutterud, Norway, where it was first found. This fine crystal was collected by the School of Mines Mission at Ihrtem, Morocco. The collection number is 16.077.

BOLEITE   This crystal originally was part of the collection of Edouard Cumenge (1828–1902), a French mining engineer. It was found in 1889 at Boleo, near Santa Rosalia, Baja California, Mexico. Boleite is composed of lead, copper, silver, and chlorine. This is the largest known crystal. Hobbyists who collect thumbnail-sized specimens (less than one inch in size) consider this to be an extraordinary crystal. The collection number is 776.

THORIANITE   This remarkable crystal is by far the largest known perfect specimen of thorianite. It weighs 2.2 kilos (nearly 5 pounds). Its main constituent is thorium, a very rare, heavy mineral. It was found in 1962 at Fort Dauphin, Malagasy Republic. The collection number is 6222.

MALACHITE (Pseudomorph after Cuprite)   This green crystal originally was a very large red cuprite crystal which over the years kept its shape but chemically changed to the green copper carbonate malachite. It is a part of the personal collection of Claude Guillemin and is on loan to the School of Mines. It was found about 1910 at Chessy, Lyons, France. The collection number is 15.724.

Nominated by John Jago, San Francisco
Photographed by Jacques Six, Paris

CERUSSITE

Collection: The Australian Museum
Curator: Oliver Chalmers
Size: 33.3 cm × 26.3 cm; 13″ × 10.5″

One of the most interesting of all of the predominately white minerals is cerussite. It forms in extremely brilliant, squatty crystals on some specimens, while other groups of crystals have grown as elongated tabular prisms. Cerussite is a heavy mineral, fairly soft, and occurs as colorless, white, or gray crystals. It was christened "cerussa" by the Romans sometime before the time of Christ. Cerussite is a secondary ore of lead. It frequently occurs in the upper levels of lead and copper mines and associates with limonite, malachite, smithsonite, azurite, phosgenite, and anglesite. It alters easily to other minerals and occurs as pseudomorphs after linarite, caledonite, leadhillite, and even ancient coins and objects made of lead. Only a few of the many localities that have produced spectacular crystals can be mentioned here: Tsumeb, South-West Africa; Sidi-Amor-ben-Salen, Tunisia; Berezovsk, Ural Mountains, U. S. S. R.; Leadhills, Lanarkshire, Scotland; Poullaouen, Brittany, France; Rezbanya, Comitat Bihar, Hungary; Wardner, Coeur d'Alene, Idaho; and the Mammoth Mines, Pinal County, Arizona.

This specimen was mined in the Proprietary Block 14 Mine, Broken Hill, New South Wales. Broken Hill, one of the early mining camps of Australia, has produced an array of colorful minerals and crystals seldom equaled anywhere in the world. Because of the aesthetic shape of its snow-white crystals, and also because of the length of the largest crystal—28.7 cm (11.5″)—this specimen is considered to be one of the best crystal groups of any species in existence.

Other fine cerussites are in the collections of Albert Chapman, Sydney, Australia; the School of Mines, Freiberg, East Germany; the School of Mines, Madrid; the School of Mines and the Faculty of Sciences in Paris; the British Museum (Natural History); the Institute of Mineralogy, Rome; the Natural History Museum, Prague; Harvard University; and the Smithsonian Institution.

Nominated by Albert Chapman, Sydney, Australia
Photographed by Charles Turner, Sydney, Australia

UVAROVITE

Collection: Professor Th. Sahama, Helsinki
Size: 19 cm × 16 cm; 7.6″ × 6.4″

Uvarovite is a member of the garnet family. Garnet occurs in many colors, including red, brown, green, yellow, white, and black, with each color having a chemical composition of its own. Uvarovite is emerald-green because a small amount of chromium exists in each crystal. Its crystals are both hard and brilliant, making gem uvarovite a much-sought-after stone. Crystals occur rarely, either in a mica schist or in solid quartz. Only a few localities have produced uvarovite, including Orford, Quebec, Canada; Pitkaranta on Lake Ladoga, Finland; Saranovskaya, Ural Mountains, U. S. S. R.; Wood's Chromite Mine, Lancaster County, Texas; and New Idria, San Benito County, California.

The uvarovite matrix pictured here was found in 1966 at Outokumpu, Finland, by Professor Sahama of the University of Helsinki. Professor Sahama recovered a large block of quartz some three hundred meters below the surface in one of Europe's largest copper mines. He hauled the twenty-five-pound chunk of quartz to the surface, after noting the presence of uvarovite crystals deeply embedded in the quartz, chrome epidote, mica, and diopside. The professor was surprised, however, to find quality crystals farther within the block, in spite of the fact that not only had the piece been badly damaged by explosives, but the remains of a drill hole still showed on the back of the quartz. After three months of chipping away the overburden of quartz, the largest and best-formed uvarovite crystals ever seen were exposed. The biggest crystal measures 4.6 cm × 2.7 cm (1.84″ × 1.1″), the second largest is a 1″ dodecahedron, and seven others exceed .5″.

Other fine uvarovite specimens are in the collections of the Smithsonian Institution; F. N. Hickernell, Cavendish, Vermont; and the School of Mines, Freiberg, East Germany.

Nominated by Frederick Pough, Santa Barbara, California
Photographed by Otso Pietinen, Helsinki

AZURITE

Collection: The Smithsonian Institution
Curator: Paul Desautels
Size: 17.9 cm × 8.3 cm; 7″ × 3.3″

This magnificent azurite crystal was discovered about 1905 at Tsumeb, South-West Africa; Tsumeb is a mining camp located in the African desert some 250 miles due north of Windhoek. The mine was discovered in 1851 and since that time has produced an unbelievable number of superb copper, lead, and zinc specimens; even today beautiful minerals are still being produced. Azurite is a copper carbonate which occasionally occurs in tabular, sharply terminated crystals of exceptional brilliance. It is usually found in the upper levels of the oxide zone as a secondary mineral. It is an important ore of copper and frequently associates with malachite, cuprite, chalcocite, limonite, and calcite. Azurite crystals are usually seen in very-dark-blue to medium-blue color and may be transparent. The mineral is too soft to be of much use in jewelry. Azurite crystals occur in copper deposits all over the world, but exceptional crystals have come from Bisbee, Arizona; Clifton, Arizona; Magdalena, Socorro County, New Mexico; Laurium, Greece; Alghero, Sardinia; Chessy, Lyons, France; Solotuschinsk, Altai, Sieria, U. S. S. R.; Moldawa, Hungary; Monts Chauves, Kielce, Poland; Wallaroo, Adelaide, and Moonta, South Australia; and Broken Hill, New South Wales, Australia. The name "azurite" comes from the Persian word "lazhward," meaning "blue."

This specimen is outstanding among many fine azurites. It was selected because of its crystal perfection, its size, and its beauty (it has partly altered to the green copper-mineral malachite). Its number is B10629.

Other outstanding azurites are in the collections of Harvard University; the American Museum of Natural History; the Fersman Mineralogy Museum, Moscow; the National Museum, Prague; the British Museum (Natural History); the School of Mines, Freiberg, East Germany; and the Museum Guimet, Lyons, France.

Nominated by Frank Gulick, Falls Church, Virginia
Photographed by Earl Lewis

EUCLASE

Collection: British Museum (Natural History)
Curator: Peter Embrey
Size: 9.6 cm $\times$ 5.1 cm; 3.8" $\times$ 2"

Euclase is a gemstone, but because of its rarity is not well-known. It has better-than-average hardness, has a bright appearance, and forms in well-terminated prismatic crystals—colorless, white, pale-green, sea-green, blue, or lavender. It is frequently transparent, and when cut, strongly resembles aquamarine and spinel. Euclase has a strong cleavage. Chemically it is a beryllium aluminum silicate. It occurs in metamorphic or pegmatite rocks. It has been found at Freiswies-alpe in Rauris-Tal, Salzburg, Austria; Gross-Glockner and Moll-Tal, Carinthia, Austria; Epprechstein and Fichtelgebirge, Bavaria, West Germany; Orenburg on the Sanarka River in the southern Ural Mountains, U. S. S. R.; a new find at Gachala, Colombia (crystals of a very rich blue); and Boa Vista, Ouro Prêto, Minas Gerais, Brazil (crystals in colors of yellow, blue, lavender, and green). At the latter locality, euclase is found with bright orange precious topaz crystals in a ratio of about one euclase to a thousand topazes.

This specimen was found in 1929 at the Lukangasi mica claim, five miles south of the Mikese railway station, Morogoro District, Tanzania. The British Museum (Natural History) purchased it from Mr. H. R. Ruggles-Brise of Norwich, England, in 1934. In that same year L. J. Spenser wrote about this exceptional crystal in the *Mining Magazine* (volume 23, page 616); a drawing of the crystal was illustrated on page 618. The large crystal is 7 cm $\times$ 4.3 cm (2.75" $\times$ 1.5") long, and all of the euclase crystals perch on a bed of mica crystals.

Other fine euclase crystals are in the collections of the American Museum of Natural History; the Fersman Mineralogical Museum, Moscow; Edward Swoboda, Los Angeles; the School of Mines, Paris; the National Museum, Prague; the Smithsonian Institution; and Harvard University.

Nominated by Charles Key, St. Petersburg, Florida
Photographed by Peter Green and Frank Greenaway

GALENA

Collection: Geological Museum, London, England
Curator: Alan Jobbins
Size: 36.1 cm × 24.4 cm; 14.2" × 9.6"

Galena is the most important ore of lead, and occasionally it forms in ore bodies having a high concentration of silver. Many galena deposits are the result of high temperature deposition. Galena is a soft but heavy mineral, with a metallic luster. It is used commercially in batteries, solder, pipes, and type metal. It forms in cubic and octahedral crystals, and, when conditions are right, thousands of crystals may grow along a single vein. These crystals usually exhibit a striking cubic cleavage. Galena is often found associated with other minerals, such as fluorite, calcite, siderite, sphalerite, pyrite, chalcopyrite, dolomite, quartz, barite, rhodonite, and even tourmaline. Exceptionally fine galena crystals have come from Santa Eulalia, Mexico; Broken Hill, New South Wales, Australia; the Tri-State mining district in the Mississippi Valley; Breckenridge, Colorado; Poullaouen, Brittany, France; Freiberg, Saxony, East Germany; Bottino, Saravezza, Tuscany, Italy; and Alston Moor, Cumberland, England. "Galena" was named after the Latin "galena," meaning "lead ore."

This unusual specimen was selected for its size, perfection and brilliance of crystals, and associative minerals siderite (brown) and calcite (white). It was found at Neudorf, Harz, Germany, in 1907; its number in the collection is M.I.769.

Other fine galenas are in the collections of Arlis Coger, Huntsville, Arkansas; the University of Copenhagen; the Natural History Museum, Vienna; the Faculty of Sciences, Paris; the School of Mines, Freiberg, East Germany; Joaquin Folch Girona, Barcelona, Spain; the British Museum (Natural History); the Royal Museum of Natural History, Stockholm; and the American Museum of Natural History.

Photographed by Martin Polsford, London
NERC Copyright, Reproduced by permission of the
Director, Institute of Geological Sciences, London, England.

CINNABAR

Collection: Mineralogical–Geological Museum, Oslo, Norway
Curator: Henrich Neumann
Size: 11 cm × 6.5 cm; 4.4″ × 2.6″

Cinnabar, the most important ore of mercury, is found in sizable deposits as a primary mineral. It occurs most frequently in slates, sandstones, limestones, and other rocks having a sedimentary origin. The pure mercury is recovered from the ore by heating, but since mercury can escape into the air as a vapor during the smelting treatment in the ovens, this process can constitute a serious health hazard to a worker who does not wear a protective shield over his nose and mouth. The color of cinnabar is red; when the crystals are transparent, the richness of its chroma can rival the ruby. Large crystals of one inch or more are rare. Good specimens have been found in the mines of Nikitovka, U. S. S. R., New Idria, California; Huancavelica, Peru; Idria, Gorizia, Italy; Mount Avala, Belgrade, Yugoslavia; Almaden, Ciudad Real, Spain; Kweichow, China; and the thousand-year-old mines of Fergana, U. S. S. R.

This specimen was chosen after one of the most difficult of the selective decisions. Nearly all major mineral museums and some private collections possess a fine example of cinnabar, but this little group of crystals demonstrated more quality, crystal perfection, and association with attendant minerals than any other judged. Many of the judges called it a "sleeper" (not a well-known specimen) and consider it to be one of the more beautiful groups of crystals in existence. The largest crystal is 4.5 cm or 1.8″ long. The flesh-colored rhombohedra are dolomite, and the brilliant-white crystals are quartz. The Oslo museum doesn't have the least idea who brought the cinnabar to the museum or the date of its arrival; it just appeared in a drawer sometime between 1895 and 1900. It has the characteristics of cinnabars that were mined at Wanshanchang, Hunan Province, China, during the nineteenth century.

Other fine groups of cinnabar crystals are in the collections of the British Museum (Natural History); Joaquin Folch Girona, Barcelona, Spain; the School of Mines, Paris; the Fersman Mineralogical Museum, Moscow; the American Museum of Natural History; the Smithsonian Institution; the Institute of Mines, Leningrad; and the School of Mines, Madrid.

Nominated by Frederick Pough, Santa Barbara, California
Photographed by Gotfred Teigen, Oslo

SIDERITE

Collection: Peter Bancroft, Ramona, California
Size: 13.7 cm × 12.2 cm; 5.3″ × 4.8″

Museum-quality siderite crystals commonly form as the background mineral for numerous specimens which display on their surfaces crystals of galena, quartz, calcite, and apatite. Siderite usually occurs in yellowish-brown to reddish-brown colors, is fairly soft, and will sometimes tarnish into a play of iridescent colors. Its crystals are rhombohedral in shape and average in size, from one-quarter of an inch to two inches and even larger; it possesses a strong cleavage in three directions. It strongly resembles calcite, but differs slightly in its chemical components and its color. Siderite is an iron carbonate commonly occurring in large shalelike sedimentary deposits. Fine crystals, for which the species is noted, are found in hydrothermal metallic veins as a primary gangue mineral. Choice siderite crystals have been found at the Morro Velho mine northwest of Ouro Prêto, Minas Gerais, Brazil; Coeur d'Alene, Idaho; Bisbee, Cochise County, Arizona; Kapnikbanya, Rumania; Freiberg, Saxony, East Germany; Val Tavetsch, Graubünden, Switzerland; Traversella, Piedmont, Italy; Pribram, Bohemia, Czechoslovakia; Erzberg, Styria, Austria; Huttenberg, Carinthia, Austria; Tavistock, Devonshire, England; St. Austell, Cornwall, England; Broken Hill, New South Wales, Australia; and, in splendid crystals covered with quartz crystals, Allevard, Isère, France.

This specimen, found at Neudorf, Germany, in the 1870s, displays water-clear quartz crystals gracefully perched atop a cluster of fine-quality siderite crystals. It was chosen because of its over-all perfection and beauty.

Other fine siderites are in the collections of the Smithsonian Institution; the School of Mines, Paris; the British Museum (Natural History); and the Museum of Natural History, Grenoble.

Nominated by Carl Stentz, Laguna Hills, California
Photographed by Earl Lewis

RUBY

Collection: British Museum (Natural History)
Curator: Peter Embrey
Size: 5.6 cm × 7.6 cm; 2.25" × 3"

Ruby is the red variety of corundum, a very hard mineral used commercially as an abrasive. When corundum is pure enough to be translucent or, preferably, transparent, it can be used as a gemstone. Blue corundum is known as sapphire. Because corundum is seldom transparent and at the same time finely colored, deep-red or blue stones are quite rare.

Ruby derives its name from the Latin "ruber" which means "red." The most desirable color in a ruby is that hue which at its richest and deepest is called "pigeon's blood." Good-quality pigeon-blood rubies weighing twenty-five carats or more are so unusual that only a few exist, and those command some of the highest prices in the entire gem world.

Most choice ruby crystals have been cut and mounted into jewelry, leaving the majority of mineral collections without a representative example. When fine ruby is displayed, it is generally in the form of a loose crystal. While most rubies were formed in metamorphic limestones, subsequent erosion of these gem deposits over the centuries has worn away the overburden and the gem crystals have settled in stream or lake beds. Thus, top-quality ruby crystals still embedded in their matrix are nearly unique. Rubies have been mined for thousands of years at Mandalay and Mogok, Burma, in a twenty-five-square-mile area. Other ruby localities are Battambang, Cambodia; Chanthaburi, Thailand; Madras, India; Campolungo, Switzerland; and various localities in Tanzania.

This ruby is not only of exceptional size and color, but it resides in its original matrix of limestone. The ruby crystal is 3.8 cm × 3.8 cm (1.5" × 1.5"). Little is known about its origin, other than that it was found at Mogok, Burma. It is not yet on display.

Other good-quality ruby crystals are in the collections of Frank P. Jaeger, New York; the Swiss Federal Institute of Technology, Zurich, Switzerland; and Harvard University.

Photographed by Peter Green and Frank Greenaway

SMALTITE

Collection: Royal Museum of Natural History, Stockholm
Size: Single crystal, 8 cm; 3.2″ (top)
    Matrix, 12 cm × 8 cm; 4.8″ × 3.2″ (bottom)

Smaltite is composed of nickel, cobalt, and arsenic; it is a basic ore of cobalt and nickel. It is usually found in veins and accompanies not only other cobalt and nickel minerals but also copper, lead, silver, zinc, and bismuth ores. It is commonly massive, and only infrequently are fine pyritohedral-shaped crystals found. Smaltite is a heavy mineral of a tin-white to steel-gray color. Cobalt is the main element in smaltite, named after the Greek "kobalos," meaning "mischievous imp." It was a troublesome mineral, always in the way, and had no value to the early miners. Modern technology has found many uses for cobalt, including its conversion to blue pigment for coloring glass and ceramics. Smaltite crystals have been found at Cobalt, Ontario, Canada; Broken Hill, New South Wales, Australia; Wheal Sparnon, Cornwall, England; Les Chalantes, France; Huelva Province, Spain; Kirkcudbrightshire, Scotland; Copiapo, Chile; and in the Transvaal of South Africa.

The single crystal pictured here (top) was mined at Hakansboda, Ramsbergs, Örebro, Sweden. It is the largest known well-formed crystal.

The matrix specimen (bottom) shows heavy striations on the cubic faces of the smaltite. The crystal is embedded in chalcopyrite and metamorphosed calcite, and is 3.3 cm × 2.5 cm (1.3″ × 1″) in size. Nearly always the smaltite crystals are broken out of the surrounding matrix during mining operations, making this piece most unusual. It was found at Tunabergs, Södermanland, Sweden.

Another fine smaltite is in the collection of the Natural History Museum, Vienna.

Nominated by John Jago, San Francisco
Photographed by K. E. Samuelsson, Stockholm

GOLDEN TOPAZ

Collection: British Museum (Natural History)
Curator: Peter Embrey
Size: 10 cm × 4.5 cm; 4.2″ × 1.8″

The colors of topaz are usually quite modest in intensity, but the subtle tints of yellow, red, orange, green, blue, and brown are so pleasing that colored topaz is highly prized as a gemstone. Topaz is quite hard and cuts into rather brilliant stones. Its crystals are most commonly prismatic; frequently the prismatic faces are heavily striated. Topaz has a strong cleavage; therefore it breaks easily and cleanly at right angles to the length of the prism. The color of some Brazilian yellow crystals may be changed to a pleasing pink simply by application of heat.

Fine topaz crystals have been found at Sverdlovsk, U. S. S. R.; Mourne Mountains, County Down, Ireland; Jos, Bauchi, Northern Nigeria; Mount Bischoff, Tasmania, Australia; Takayama, Honshū, Japan; various streams in Ceylon; San Luis Potosi, Mexico; Villa Rica, Minas Gerais, Brazil; Florissant, Colorado; and Ramona, San Diego County, California.

This topaz crystal was selected to represent the golden or "precious" species of topaz. It possesses unusual size, clarity, crystal perfection, and color. It was found at Ouro Prêto, Minas Gerais, Brazil, about 1832, and was collected by Mr. Henry Heuland in 1833. In 1834 Heuland sold it to an Englishman named Walker; many years later it found its way to the British Museum (Natural History) as part of the Walker Collection. In 1893 Walker wrote an article in which he said, "This is the finest yellow topaz known."

Other notable golden topaz crystals are in the collections of the National Museum, Rio de Janeiro, Brazil; the Los Angeles County Museum, Los Angeles; the School of Mines, Paris; the Institute of Mineralogy, Florence, Italy; and the National Museum, Prague.

Nominated by Charles Key, St. Petersburg, Florida
Photographed by Peter Green and Frank Greenaway

AQUAMARINE MATRIX

Collection: The Smithsonian Institution
Curator: Paul Desautels
Size: 30 cm × 17.5 cm; 12″ × 7″

Aquamarines are found either as water-worn pebbles in stream beds or as crystals which are usually broken from their rocky homes in mines in order for the miner to recover the maximum amount of cutting material. Very seldom are fine-quality aquamarine crystals kept intact in their matrixes. This specimen, known as the "boat" or "ship," is the outstanding example of an aquamarine matrix. While the aquamarine crystals are neither of deep color nor of superior clarity, still from an aesthetic viewpoint this specimen is rated by many collectors as one of the best in the world. The associated minerals are attractively arranged and are well-formed. The shiny white hexagonal crystal is muscovite (white mica), the black crystals are tourmaline, and the small whitish crystals are albite. This association or gathering of different and contrasting crystals has resulted in this glamorous cluster being rated unique.

This specimen was mined at Palmital, Minas Gerais, Brazil, in 1951. Alfredo Heuberg, co-owner of Inter-Ocean Trade Company of New York City, purchased the specimen in Brazil and brought it by hand to Washington, D. C., where he sold it to the Smithsonian. It was purchased with Roebling funds (R9163 of the Roebling Collection) and is on display in the mineral hall of the Smithsonian Institution.

Other top-quality aquamarine matrixes are to be seen in the collections of the Fersman Mineralogical Museum, Moscow; the School of Mines and the Faculty of Sciences, Paris; the Civic Museum of Natural History, Milan; and the Institute of Mines, Leningrad.

Nominated by Edward Swoboda, Los Angeles
Photographed by Earl Lewis

ORTHOCLASE

Collection: University of Milan, Institute of Mineralogy
Curator: Bona Potenza Bianchi
Size: 25.2 cm $\times$ 21.3 cm; 10" $\times$ 8.4"

A representative of the orthoclase-feldspar group is illustrated here because it is one of the most important of the rock-forming minerals. Orthoclase is also the most common of all of the silicate minerals. It occurs in stocky prismatic crystals which quite frequently "twin" as Carlsbad or Baveno crystals. Such a twin results when two crystals are so intergrown that some of the crystal faces are common to both crystals while other faces protrude from the specimen to separate clearly one crystal from the other. Most orthoclase crystals are colorless, white, yellowish, or reddish. Orthoclase is about average in hardness; crystal faces can be quite brilliant to the light. Fine crystals have been found in pegmatite veins at Pfitschtal, Trentino, Italy; La Colta, the island of Elba, Italy; Puy-de-Dôme, France; Frederiksvärn, Vestfold, Norway; St. Agnes, Cornwall, England; Pingau, Salzburg, Austria; Itrongahy, Betroka, Malagasy Republic; Takayama, Japan; Mount Antero, Chaffee County, Colorado; Barringer Hill, Llano County, Texas; Mesa Grande, California; and Good-springs, Nevada.

This very fine specimen consists of a mixture of orthoclase and quartz crystals. Frequently such specimens are found high in the mountains and near the surface where the spring thaws sometimes crack and destroy the crystals. An undamaged specimen, such as this one, is a rarity. These orthoclase crystals are excellent examples of Baveno twinning. Associate minerals on the matrix are calcite, apatite, calcite (yellow), and muscovite. The largest orthoclase crystal is 6.1 cm (2.5" long). It was found in 1920 at a pink granite quarry at Baveno near Lake Maggiore, Italy. It became a part of the Collezione Bazzi which was sold to the institute in 1930.

Nearly every European museum displays a fine orthoclase from Italy. Notable examples are in the collections of the Faculty of Sciences and the School of Mines, both in Paris.

Nominated by Giuseppe Vergato, Rome
Photographed by Dr. G. H. Crespi, University of Milan, Institute of Mineralogy

HIDDENITE

Collection: Cranbrook Institute of Science, Bloomfield Hills, Michigan
Director: Warren L. Wittry
Size: 4.5 cm × .96 cm, 1.5″ × .4″

The grass-green variety of spodumene is known as hiddenite. Spodumene is a lithium, aluminum silicate which grows into crystals perhaps weighing only a few grams or giants weighing ninety tons. The very large crystals have little commercial value but are of considerable interest because of their enormous size. Occasionally the smaller crystals occur as clear, heavily striated prisms in colors of yellow, pink, or (rarely) green. Crystals of these colors cut into beautiful, limpid stones which, because of their rarity, are better known to the collector than to the jewelry trade. Spodumene is fairly hard, and its luster is quite bright. Yellow stones are known as yellow spodumene; the pink as kunzite; the rich chrome-green variety as hiddenite. Lighter-colored green spodumenes are called green spodumene, not hiddenite. Hiddenite has been found primarily at small mines near Stony Point, Alexander County, North Carolina. Hiddenite was named for Mr. W. E. Hidden.

This hiddenite crystal is exceptional because of its size (hiddenite crystals seldom exceed one inch in length), perfection of crystal shape, and interplay of yellow and green colors. It was acquired by the Cranbrook Institute of Science in 1939. This hiddenite specimen is a marvelous example of a miniature crystal. (Miniatures must fit inside a two-inch cube when entered in mineral display competition.)

Other fine hiddenite crystals are in the collections of Harvard University; the Natural History Museum, Vienna; William Larson, Fallbrook, California; and the Smithsonian Institution.

Nominated by Rock Currier, Ardsley, New York
Photographed by Earl Lewis

MALACHITE (Pseudomorph after Azurite)

Collection: Gerhard Becker
Size: 19 cm × 11.3 cm; 7.6″ × 4.5″

Malachite crystals are very rare. When good-sized crystals appear to be malachite, they nearly always are pseudomorphed after some other mineral; that is, the shape of the host mineral is retained, but the new mineral (malachite) has replaced the original mineral. Malachite forms in the upper levels of copper mines, most frequently in the oxidized mineral zone as a secondary and minor ore of copper. Massive malachite is found as banded layers of bright green material, which over the years has been cut and carved into desk sets, vases, lamp bases, figurines, and cabochon stones for jewelry. The largest known block of gem malachite, measuring a reported 9 by 18 feet, was mined about 1820 at Nizhni-Tagil, near Sverdlovsk, U. S. S. R. This block is supposed to have produced 250 tons of top-grade cutting material. Fine malachite pseudomorphs after cuprite are found at Chessy, Lyons, France; after atacamite and brochantite, from Broken Hill, New South Wales, Australia; after calcite, azurite, and cerussite, from Tsumeb, South-West Africa; and after azurite, from Bisbee, Arizona.

This outstanding specimen displays an exotic array of malachite crystals pseudomorphed after azurite and tufted with quartz crystals backed by massive bands of malachite. Most malachite crystals associate with other copper and lead minerals. Malachite with quartz is an uncommon occurrence, and a specimen approaching the quality of these crystals is extremely rare. It was found at Zacatecas, Mexico, about 1910.

Other fine crystal specimens of malachite pseudomorphs are in the collections of the Smithsonian Institution; the Fersman Mineralogical Museum, Moscow; E. M. Gunnell, Denver, Colorado; the School of Mines, Freiberg, East Germany; and Harvard University.

Nominated by Gunter Fuchs, Karlsruhe, West Germany
Photographed by Karl Hartmann

ANATASE

Collection: British Museum (Natural History)
Curator: Peter Embrey
Size: 13.4 cm × 9.5 cm; 5.3″ × 3.8″

Anatase is quite a rare mineral, especially when found in fine crystals. It is a titanium mineral which forms in stocky pyramids. Its color ranges through various shades of brown into blue and black. It has average hardness, has quite a brilliant luster, is brittle, and has a pronounced cleavage. It occurs in detritus deposits and as such can have a commercial value as a titanium ore. Crystals usually occur in veins in metamorphic schists and gneisses which exist in the Alpine regions. Crystals of more than .5″ are quite rare. Anatase associates with hematite, rutile, brookite, chlorite, apatite, quartz, and adularia. Good crystals have been found at La Grave, Hautes-Alpes, France; Griesiwies, Rauris, Salzburg, Austria; Sondalo, Lombardy, Italy; Cavradi, Tavetsch, Graubünden, Switzerland; the Virtuous Lady Mine, Tavistock, Devonshire, England; Sanarka, Orenburg, U. S. S. R.; Diamantina, Minas Gerais, Brazil; and Beaver Creek, Gunnison County, Colorado.

This specimen has the largest known well-formed anatase crystal perched in a bed of calcite crystals. The crystal measures 3.75 cm × 3.25 cm (1.5″ × 1.3″). It was found at Binn, Valais, Switzerland, in about 1896. It was sold to the British Museum (Natural History) by F. Krantz of Bonn, Germany, in 1900.

Other fine anatase crystals are in the collections of the Smithsonian Institution; the Faculty of Sciences, Paris; the Swiss Federal Institute of Technology, Zurich; the University of Copenhagen; and the Natural History Museum, Vienna.

Nominated by Charles Key, St. Petersburg, Florida
Photographed by Peter Green and Frank Greenaway

RHODOCHROSITE (Pseudomorph after Calcite)

Collection: Natural History Museum, Paris
Size: 32 cm × 24 cm; 12.8″ × 9.6″

This beautiful specimen is an extraordinary example of pseudomorphosis, wherein the original mineral (calcite) left its distinct crystal form and was replaced by a new mineral, the pink rhodochrosite. Thus, this specimen illustrates the typical characteristics of rhodochrosite—pink color, a greater hardness and weight than calcite, and a chemical composition primarily composed of manganese—but it will retain forever the original form of its calcite host. It was coated lightly at a later time in its history by a light crust of tiny colorless quartz crystals. There are a number of small pyrite crystals down one side of the matrix.

This specimen was mined at Kassandra, Greece, in 1966. It was first collected by a Monsieur Gauthier and was donated to the Paris Natural History Museum in 1967. It is now in the foyer of the museum and is listed as a "recent acquisition."

Rhodochrosite is a minor ore of manganese, but has produced exotic clusters of crystals in a wide variety of colors, ranging from bright-red to lavender to yellow. It was formed in low-temperature veins of silver, copper, lead, and zinc ores. Its name is derived from the Greek "rose color." Rhodochrosite is also known as dialogite in some countries.

A 21 cm × 17 cm portion of the specimen is shown in this photograph. The largest crystal is 6.5 cm × 4 cm (2.6″ × 1.6″).

The judges knew of no other rhodochrosite pseudomorph of exceptional quality, and no other was nominated.

Nominated by H. J. Schubnel, Paris
Photographed by Jacques Six

WITHERITE

Collection: British Museum (Natural History)
Curator: Peter Embrey
Size: 10 cm × 8.8 cm; 4″ × 3.6″

Witherite is a rather rare barium mineral. It is fairly soft and has a rich luster. Its color is usually white—milky, grayish, or colorless. Occasionally it may be lightly tinted yellow, green, or brown. Witherite easily fluoresces under X rays or ultraviolet light. It is commonly found in low-temperature hydrothermal veins associated with galena and, occasionally, barite. It may have been formed by crystallization from barium-carbonate-saturated waters, or by carbonated waters acting upon barite. Witherite crystallizes into stocky, twinned hexagonally shaped crystals the faces of which are generally rough and sometimes striated.

Witherite crystals were first discovered at Alston Moor, Cumberland, England. Later they were found at Leogang, Salzburg, Austria; the Himmelsfurst Mine, Freiberg, East Germany; the Maximilian Mine, Andreasberg, Saxony, East Germany; Dyalankol, North Caucasus, U. S. S. R; Pribram, Bohemia, Czechoslovakia; Château Thinieres, Beaulieu, Cantal, France; Rosiclare, Hardin County, Illinois; and Castle Dome, Yuma County, Arizona.

This specimen was collected personally in January 1931 by the late Sir Arthur Russell, eminent British mineralogist. He found the specimen in a large cavity of the Liverick Vein, in the crosscut between Treloar and the High Raise Vein, in the Nentsberry mine at Alston, Cumberland, England. Sir Arthur Russell bequeathed the specimen to the British Museum (Natural History) in 1964.

This witherite is invested with and partly altered to barite. The largest crystal is 3.3 cm × 2.3 cm (1.3″ × .9″). Its number in the collection is BM 1964R.

Another fine witherite is in the collection of the School of Mines, Paris.

Nominated by Charles Key, St. Petersburg, Florida
Photographed by Peter Green and Frank Greenaway

SPANGOLITE

Collection: Edward Swoboda, Los Angeles, California
Size: 14 cm × 12.7 cm; 5.5″ × 5″

Spangolite is a very rare copper-and-aluminum mineral. It was first found near Tombstone, Cochise County, Arizona, in 1889. It was just eight years earlier that United States Marshal Wyatt Earp and his deputies brought Tombstone world-wide fame by killing three desperadoes in the famous gunfight at the O.K. Corral. While spangolite crystals did not attract similar attention, they were recognized as a new mineral. Later other spangolite specimens were found in the Metcalf mine near Clifton, Greenlee County, Arizona. Crystals were also found at Majuba Hill, Pershing County, Nevada; the Grand Central mine, Tintic, Utah; St. Day, Cornwall, England; and Arenas, Iglesias, Sardinia, Italy. Crystals are extremely rare, but do form in hexagonal, tabular shapes. The color of spangolite varies from emerald green to dark green. Spangolite was named after Norman Spang of Etna, Pennsylvania, who first suspected that his specimen represented a new species.

This spangolite specimen contains the largest and best-formed known crystals in matrix. The major crystal is 1.6 cm long (.63″). The spangolite crystals lie imbedded in a nest of minute malachite crystals. The brown streaks surrounding the green vug are limonite; the bright-red specks are cuprite. It was found in the famous Copper Queen Mine at Bisbee, Arizona.

Another fine spangolite is in the British Museum (Natural History).

Nominated by Rock Currier, Ardsley, New York
Photographed by Earl Lewis

MEDIA SERVICES
EVANSTON TOWNSHIP HIGH SCHOOL

143017

STIBNITE

Collection: David Wilber, Reno, Nevada
Size: 20.30 cm × 12.7 cm; 8″ × 5″

Stibnite is one of the most spectacular minerals in the world of crystals. Its long, heavily striated, silver-to-jet-black prisms attain a grandeur that no other black crystal can match. In a fine piece each crystal stands erect with an éclat and definition that is typical of the mineral. Stibnite as the major source of antimony forms at low temperatures in hydrothermal ore bodies. The refined metal melts at relatively low temperatures and thus can be used in alloys to be cast into storage battery plates, pewter, and printing type. Its by-products are used in the manufacture of rubber, pigments, medicines, matches, and fireworks. In ancient times it served as a cosmetic eye shadow. Stibnite associates with pyrite, cinnabar, barite, realgar, orpiment, ankerite, galena, marcasite, calcite, and quartz. It is found at Felsöbánya and Kapnik, Rumania; Pereta, Tuscany, Italy; Freiberg, Saxony, East Germany; Kremnitz, Czechoslovakia; Lubilhac, Haute-Loire, France; Bau, Sarawak, Borneo; and Manhattan, Toquima Range, south central Nevada. Especially noteworthy are the superb crystals of the Ichinokawa mine, Niihama City, Ehime Prefecture, Japan.

Nearly every major collection has a Japanese stibnite, for Japan has been prolific in producing many of the best stibnites in the world.

This very fine stibnite is rather small when compared to the 18″ to 20″ shafts of the Japanese stibnites. However, for sheer beauty of form, a substantial number of the judges felt it to be superior to any other stibnite specimen. These brilliant crystals are attached to a base of limestone. This stibnite was mined at Kisbanya, Rumania, in 1946.

Fine stibnites are to be seen in the collections of the British Museum (Natural History); the Peabody Museum, Yale University; the American Museum of Natural History; Teyler's Museum, Haarlem, The Netherlands; Edward Swoboda, Los Angeles; the Mitsubishi Metal Mining Company Museum, Omiya, Japan; the University of Tokyo; and Harvard University.

Nominated by George Holloway, Northridge, California
Photographed by Earl Lewis

AUTUNITE

Collection: The Smithsonian Institution
Curator: Paul Desautels
Size: 11.7 cm × 5.6 cm; 4.5″ × 2.25″

Autunite is a secondary ore of uranium and is formed by the altering of uraninite or other uranium-bearing minerals. It is relatively soft, has a pearly luster, and its color ranges throughout the greens and yellows. Autunite is highly fluorescent in ultraviolet light. Its crystals are thin and tabular, are frequently malformed, and sometimes are foliated aggregates. Autunite is very radioactive. The uranium element when separated from autunite is important as a material used in atomic energy work, especially in the isotope U-235 which is capable of continuous fission. Autunite was named after Autun, France (a well-known mining district), located about 170 miles southeast of Paris.

Autunite is found at Kolwezi, Zaire; Antsirabe, Malagasy Republic; St. Austell, Cornwall, England; Saint-Symphorien, Saône-et-Loire, France; Falkenstein and Johanngeorgenstadt, Saxony, East Germany; Viseu, Portugal; and Spokane, Washington.

This specimen of autunite was mined at Margnac, France, and was obtained by the Smithsonian Institution through exchange with the University of Paris, with the assistance of Dr. Pierre Bariand. Its number in the Smithsonian Collection is 120743.

Other fine autunites are in the collections of Joseph Urban, Tucson, Arizona; the School of Mines, Paris; and David Wilber, Reno, Nevada.

Nominated by John Jago, San Francisco
Photographed by Earl Lewis

PHOSGENITE

Collection: Joaquin Folch Girona, Barcelona, Spain
Size: 11.5 cm × 11 cm; 4.6″ × 4.4″

Phosgenite is a rather heavy mineral which chemically is a chlorocarbonate of lead. It comes in pastel shades of pink, green, brown, or yellow. Frequently crystals are colorless or white. Crystals of phosgenite occur rarely in lead mines. Specimens of notable size have been collected at Tarnowitz, Poland; Altai, Siberia, U. S. S. R.; Cromford, Derbyshire, England; Montevecchio and Gibbas, Sardinia, Italy; and Tsumeb, South-West Africa. It was named from the word "phosgen," which describes the chemical carbonyl chloride. One of the most interesting occurrences of phosgenite is at Laurium, Greece. The Greeks created new minerals without being aware of the process or of the results. They operated a great silver-lead mine at Laurium hundreds of years before the birth of Christ and dumped its waste into the Mediterranean Sea. The salty waters leached away some of the mineralized slag and rearranged the chemical composition to form new minerals, among them fiedlerite, penfieldite, laurionite, and, of course, phosgenite.

This superb crystal of phosgenite was mined at Monteponi, near Iglesias, Sardinia, Italy, in 1955. It was purchased in 1965 from Martin Ehrmann who had obtained it from a collector in Milan. This specimen is unusual for its combination of size, crystal perfection, clarity, and light-brown color.

Other fine phosgenite crystals are displayed in the collections of the School of Mines, Paris; the Civic Museum of Natural History, Milan; and the American Museum of Natural History.

Nominated by Charles Key, St. Petersburg, Florida
Photographed by Francisco Bedmar

CHALCOCITE

Collection: British Museum (Natural History)
Curator: Peter Embrey
Size: 7.1 cm × 6.3 cm; 2.8″ × 2.5″

Chalcocite is one of the most important ores of copper and is quite common. It is usually found in heavy sulfide deposits deep in copper mines, but fine crystals have also been discovered in the oxide zones of the upper levels. Chalcocite forms in short, prismatic crystals, frequently as twins, but good crystals are very rare. It is colored grayish-black and is a heavy mineral. It associates with covellite, malachite, cuprite, azurite, pyrite, chalcopyrite, and bornite. Occasionally small amounts of silver occur with chalcocite. For many years chalcocite was called "Copper Glance."

Chalcocite crystals have been found at Redruth, Cornwall, England; Bogolosvk, Ural Mountains, U. S. S. R.; Joachimsthal, Bohemia, Czechoslovakia; Dognacska, Rumania; Tsumeb, South-West Africa; (near) Mindouli, Congo; Butte, Montana; Bristol, Connecticut; and Kennecott on the Copper River, Alaska.

This splendid matrix was found in the Levant Mine, Cornwall, in 1899. It was sold to the British Museum (Natural History) by Mr. W. Semmons of London in 1905. The major crystal is 4.5 cm (1.8″) long. Some collectors and curators rate this classic piece as the best small mineral specimen in the world. The mineral's number is 1905–207.

Other fine chalcocites are in the collections of the Museum of Central Africa, Tervuren, Belgium; the School of Mines, the Faculty of Sciences, and the Natural History Museum, all in Paris; the Geological Museum, London; the Smithsonian Institution; Harvard University; the American Museum of Natural History; and William Pinch, Rochester, New York.

Nominated by C. Douglas Woodhouse, Santa Barbara, California
Photographed by Peter Green and Frank Greenaway

MORGANITE

Collection: David Wilber, Reno, Nevada
Size: 8.1 cm × 7.9 cm; 3.2″ × 3.1″

Morganite is the pink variety of beryl. Other members of the beryl family are aquamarine, the blue to blue-green variety; golden beryl, which is the yellow variety; and emerald, the dark-green variety. Morganite may be colored pale pink to rose-red, with most crystals holding to the lighter shades. Some morganite occurs in an apricot color. Morganite, because of its delicate color, ample hardness, comparative rarity, and brilliance, is quite popular in jewelry. It is cut in square, emerald, and brilliant shapes, and usually is not a very expensive stone. Morganite has been found as excellent crystals at Ampangabe, and Marharitra, Mount Bity, Malagasy Republic; near Teofilo Otoni, Minas Gerais, Brazil; at Mesa Grande, and at the Katrina and Pala Queen mines at Pala, San Diego County, California. Morganite was named after the American financier J. P. Morgan, who loved minerals and who endowed the famous Morgan gem collection at the American Museum of Natural History.

This specimen is a superb example of a gem crystal. It is doubly terminated, has good color, is of excellent quality, is without damage, and rests on a bed of white cleavelandite crystals. It was found in 1964 in the White Queen mine located on Harriart Mountain just northeast of Pala. It was found at the bottom of a large pocket and was covered by between nine and ten tons of quartz crystals. This same pocket produced more than 250 pounds of morganite, much of it of gem quality. The White Queen was discovered in 1900, but development was confined to the northern end of the claim, which the present owner, Norman Dawson of San Marcos, California, bought in 1946. A short while later his wife, Vi, discovered a small aquamarine crystal on a trail. At that point a tunnel was started into the mountain, and, five feet inside, enough blue tourmaline crystals were found to fill a wheelbarrow. The mine has also produced blue apatite, columbite, stilbite, lepidolite, bismuthinite, citrine, smoky quartz, and montmorillonite.

Other fine morganites are in the collections of the National Museum, Prague; the Smithsonian Institution; Harvard University; the J. P. Morgan Collection at the American Museum of Natural History; the School of Mines, the Faculty of Sciences, and the Natural History Museum, all in Paris; the British Museum (Natual History); the Institute of Mineralogy, Rome; the Fersman Mineralogical Museum, Moscow, and the Feire de Andrade Museum, Lourenço Marques, Mozambique.

Nominated by George Holloway, Northridge, California
Photographed by Earl Lewis

SMOKY QUARTZ

Collection: Peter Indergand, Göschenen, Switzerland
Size: 90 cm × 60 cm; 36″ × 16″

Quartz occurs abundantly all over the world. In fact, it is the most common of all minerals. The brownish variety of quartz, known as smoky quartz, is also quite common. Gem-quality smoky quartz is prized for cutting material, and fine crystals are popular features of mineral and gem collections. Exceptional smoky quartz crystals have been found at Cairngorm, Banffshire, Scotland; Betafo, Malagasy Republic; Rio Grande do Sul, Brazil; Guanajuato, Mexico; Mursinsk, Ural Mountains, U. S. S. R.; Pikes Pike, Colorado; and various localities near St. Gotthard, Switzerland.

This magnificent group of crystals was found in 1946 by Peter Indergand, Sr., at the Furka Pass near the Tiefengletscher, Switzerland, at an elevation of 8400 feet. It was located in a 3′ × 24′ granite cavity that was nearly filled with ice. It took many weeks for Indergand to bring his prize over the glaciers to the valley below; this arduous task resulted in his premature death. The crystal cluster weighs 180 kilos (about 470 pounds) and may be seen resting on its bed of granite pebbles in the little museum and souvenir shop (managed by Peter Indergand, Jr.) in Göschenen, Switzerland.

Other fine smoky quartz specimens include a five-ton crystal in the Civic Museum, Belo Horizonte, Brazil; a large group of crystals in the Natural History Museum, Bern; in the Fersman Mineralogical Museum, Moscow; in the collection of H. Huguenin-Stadler, Cafe-Konditorie Kristall, Altdorf, Switzerland; and in the Municipal Museum, Idar-Oberstein, West Germany.

Nominated by Valentin Sicher, Gurtnellen, Switzerland
Photographed by Willi Guyer, Klingnau, Switzerland

DIAMOND

Collection: The Smithsonian Institution
Curator: Paul Desautels
Size: 5.14 cm × 5.1 cm; 2″ × 2″

The diamond is the hardest of all gemstones. This hardness prevented a widespread use of the diamond until relatively recent times, because there was no known way to fashion the stone into desirable shapes. Diamonds, when used in jewelry, were usually set in their natural crystal state, until techniques were developed wherein diamonds could be cleaved and faceted into the beautiful stones we now know. Since nearly all large diamonds are cut into gemstones, most museums display glass models of oversized crystals which no longer exist. The largest diamond crystal ever found was the Cullinan with a weight of 3025 carats and a very irregular shape. Probably less than a dozen diamond crystals have weighed more than 200 carats when found, and of these only one, named the Oppenheimer, remains as a natural crystal. Even though most diamonds are white or yellowish in color, fine crystals have been found with green, blue, orange, red, or brown colors. Diamonds usually form as octahedrons (eight-sided crystals).

The superb quality yellowish diamond displayed here is the Oppenheimer. It was found at Dutoitspan, South Africa, weighs 253.7 carats, and is of exceptionally fine quality. It was given to the Smithsonian Institution by the New York jewelry firm of Harry Winston, Inc., in memory of Sir Ernest Oppenheimer. It is not only the largest but also the finest diamond crystal in existence. The Colenso diamond, weighing 133 carats and once a part of the British Museum (Natural History) Collection, has been stolen.

Important diamond localities are Kimberley, De Beers, Bulfontein, and Dutoitspan Mines in South Africa; Bushimaie, Zaire; Mudgee, New South Wales, Australia; Diamantina, Minas Gerais, Brazil; and Murfreesboro, Pike County, Arkansas.

Nominated by Edward Owens, New York City
Photographed by Earl Lewis

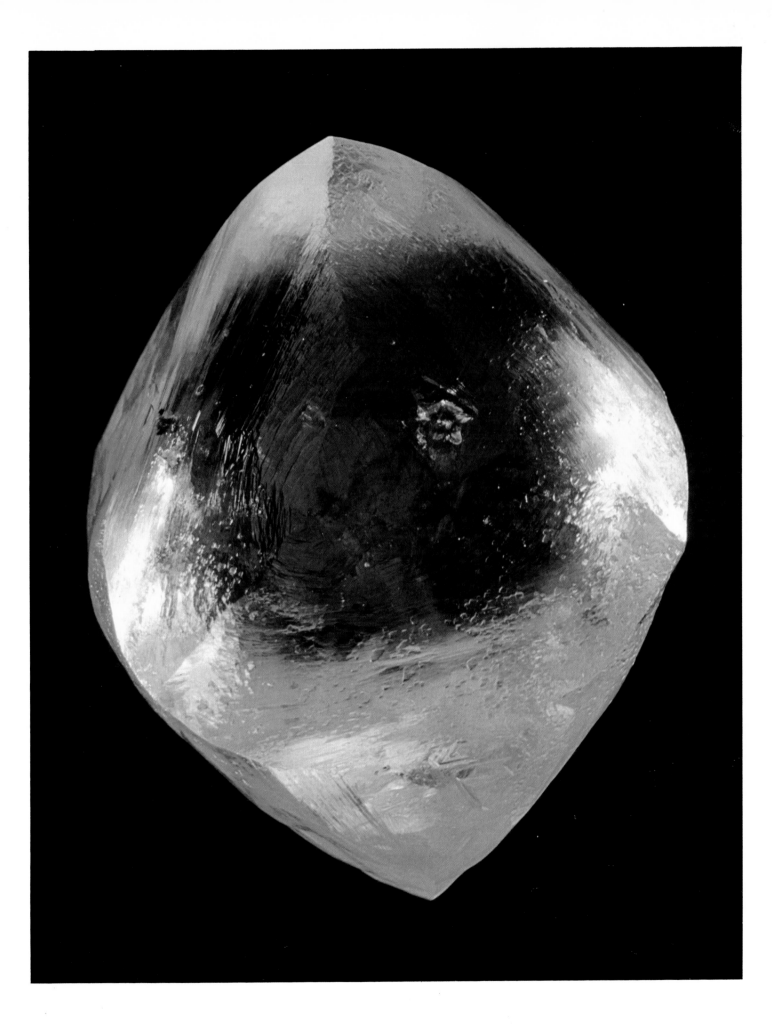

SMITHSONITE (Reniform)

Collection: Roger Williams, Encino, California
Size: 25.4 cm × 20.3 cm; 10″ × 8.1″

Smithsonite is a zinc carbonate which frequently occurs as a brownish mass. Occasionally it is found as a blue or green reniform (kidney-shaped) mass; only rarely does it grow as a crystal. In Europe it is referred to as calamine, but the most accepted name is smithsonite. It was named after the wealthy Englishman James Smithson, who willed a sizable portion of his estate to establish the Smithsonian Institution. Years ago smithsonite was fashioned into blue and green stones for jewelry, but its softness soon diminished its popularity. Fine reniform masses have been found at the fabulous silver, lead, and zinc mines at Laurium, Greece, which were worked as early as 3000 years ago by the Phoenicians. Other localities are Bleiberg, Carinthia, Austria; St. Laurent du Minier in Herault, France; Aachen, West Germany; Altenberg, Belgium; Iglesias, Sardinia, Italy; Granby, Missouri; Leadville, Colorado; and Marion County, Arkansas.

This superb specimen was discovered in the Kelly Mine, Magdalena County, New Mexico. It is considered the largest, best-formed blue-green smithsonite in existence. The piece is partially hollow, but the top and the entire circumference are without damage. Roger Williams, internationally known pianist and an avid mineral collector, considers this smithsonite to be the choicest mineral in his collection.

Other fine reniform smithsonites are in the collections of the Smithsonian Institution; the School of Mines, Paris; and David Wilber, Reno, Nevada.

Nominated by William Larson, Fallbrook, California
Photographed by Earl Lewis

WOLFRAMITE

Collection: Harvard University
Curator: Clifford Frondel
Size: 16.5 cm × 15.2 cm; 6.5" × 6"

Wolframite, one of the principal ores of tungsten, usually contains some iron and manganese. Its rare crystals are usually tabular or prismatic in shape. Its color varies from grayish to brownish to iron-black. It is of medium hardness and is quite heavy. Wolframite associates commonly with cassiterite, arsenopyrite, quartz, tourmaline, and hematite. Important deposits of wolframite occur at Ehrenfriedersdorf, Saxony, East Germany; Schlaggenwald, Bohemia, Czechoslovakia; Felsobanya, Rumania; Adervielle, Hautes-Pyrénées, France; Panasqueira, Portugal; Transbaikalia, U. S. S. R.; Cornwall, England; Mawchi, Burma; Ardlethan, New South Wales, Australia; Llallagua, Bolivia; Sierra de Cordoba, Argentina; Picuris, Taos County, New Mexico; and the world's most extensive deposit, the Nanling Range in southern China.

In this beautiful specimen the black wolframite crystals are associated with a spray of iron-stained quartz crystals. It was mined at Chicote Grande, Inquisivi, Bolivia, in 1925. Inquisivi is a remote mining camp perched high on the side of the Bolivian Andes. It is surrounded by giant peaks ranging between 19,000 and 21,000 feet in height. In the rarefied air mining is particularly difficult, but the mines of the area have produced some of the most superb tungsten and tin crystals known. This specimen was collected by Senor Ahlfeld of La Paz, Bolivia. In 1932 the Ahlfeld Collection, which included the wolframite, was sold to Harvard University. The largest wolframite crystal is 2.5 cm × 5.0 cm (1" × 2"). Its number in the Harvard Collection is 91690.

Other fine wolframite specimens are in the collections of the School of Mines, Freiberg, East Germany; the School of Mines and the Faculty of Sciences, both of Paris; the Faculty of Sciences, Porto, Portugal; the National Museum, Prague; the Fersman Mineralogical Museum, Moscow; and David Wilber, Reno, Nevada.

Nominated by Rock Currier, Ardsley, New York
Photographed by Earl Lewis

REALGAR

Collection: Edward Swoboda, Los Angeles, California
Size: 15.3 cm × 23.4 cm; 6.1″ × 9.2″

Realgar, with its bright red color, is one of the most beautiful of all minerals, but it is also one of the most deadly. Because the chemical composition is arsenic mono-sulfide, derivatives of realgar are used as insecticides and weed killers. Realgar is very soft, and while it may be transparent when it first comes from the mine, long exposure to light will cause disintegration until it becomes a powder. Realgar associates with antimony, gold, silver, lead, and other arsenic ores. It also occurs as a volcanic sublimation residue, and as a deposit from hot springs. Crystals of good quality are quite unusual; when removed from the mine wall, they frequently will fracture in all directions. Therefore, because of the mineral's fragility and instability, fine crystal groups are generally not on exhibit. Good crystals have been reported from the Getchell mine, Golconda, Nevada; Mercury, Tooele County, Utah; Monte Cristo, Snohomish County, Washington; Shimotsuke, Japan; Pozzuoli, Naples, Italy; Binnental, Valais, Switzerland; and at Nagyàg, Transylvania, Rumania.

This magnificent specimen was mined by Mr. Bart Cannon, in 1972, at Green River Gorge, Franklin, King County, Washington. Edward Swoboda obtained it in October of the same year. It contains the largest perfect crystal ever found, measuring 5.3 cm (2.1″) in length.

Other fine specimens are in the collections of the Museum of Natural History, Vienna, and the Smithsonian Institution.

Photographed by Van Pelt, Los Angeles

MAGNETITE

Collection: The National Museum, Prague
Director: Karel Tucek
Curator: Jaroslav Svenek
Size: 14.7 cm × 9.9 cm; 5.8″ × 3.9″

Magnetite is the magnetic iron ore. It is of medium hardness, is jet-black in color, and is very heavy. Mammoth deposits exist at Kiruna, Sweden, where reserves are estimated at 1.3 billion tons. The Greek philosopher Theophrastus wrote a book in 300 B.C. in which he described this heavy mineral as "the stone that attracts iron." Magnetite has continued to intrigue scientists and laymen alike ever since. But crystals of exceptional size and quality are very rare, with the best crystals usually found in the clefts of the Alps. Good-quality magnetite crystals occur at Falun and Nordmark, Sweden; Vasco, Rumania; Achmatovsk, Zlatoust, Ural Mountains, U. S. S. R.; Zillertal, Tyrol, Austria; Chillagoe, Queensland, Australia; and Itabira, Minas Gerais, Brazil.

This fine crystal, which is embedded in mica schist and is associated with quartz and dolomite crystals, was found in the 1910s at Alp Lercheltiny, southwest of St. Gotthard Pass, Switzerland. The size of the crystal is 5.1 cm × 4.1 cm (2″ × 1.6″). Its collection number is 2065. This specimen is one of many prizes in the collection of Prague's National Museum, located at one end of Wenceslaus Square. The collection contains specimens mined more than two hundred years ago. The display includes fine Bohemian and Rumanian minerals, including hessite, nagyagite, and stephanite. This museum is one of the most ornate in the world, possessing a huge open area in the center of the building, which is five stories high. Carpeted steps seat hundreds of people who each week come to listen beneath the marble columns to orchestras and vocal groups.

Fine magnetites are to be seen in the collections of the School of Mines and Natural History Museum, Paris; the Institute of Mineralogy, Turin, Italy; the Royal Museum of Natural History, Stockholm; and Harvard University.

Nominated by Jaroslav Svenek, Prague, Czechoslovakia
Photographed by Frantisek Tvrz, Prague

NATIVE SILVER

Collection: Peter Bancroft, Ramona, California
Size: 16.5 cm × 11.4 cm; 6.5″ × 4.5″

This specimen of native silver was mined at Kongsberg, Norway, in 1878. Native silver is found as nearly pure silver in the mines. This specimen is neither the largest nor the heaviest of the wire silvers in existence, but it was chosen because of its beauty and its association with calcite. The bottom of the specimen is formed about a cluster of calcite crystals; the bluish mineral nearby is a silver sulfide named acanthite, and the copper-appearing mineral is native copper.

The Kongsberg Silver Mine was discovered in 1623 and is one of Norway's oldest mines. King Christian IV claimed the mine as belonging to the Crown and imported German miners to develop it. Soon Kongsberg was the largest Norwegian city, and by 1771 there were eighty silver mines in operation.

Today nearly all of the mines are shut down because the high-grade ore is gone, but these mines did produce 1350 tons of pure silver during their history.

Native silver is much rarer in occurrence than native gold, but it is widely distributed in small amounts. Most of the world's fine silvers are from Kongsberg, but noteworthy specimens have been found at Freiberg, Saxony, East Germany; Pribram, Bohemia, Czechoslovakia; Atacama, Chile; Ontario, Canada; Aspen, Colorado; and numerous localities in Mexico.

Other fine silver specimens are in the collections of the University of Copenhagen; the Mining Museum, Kongsberg; the Geology Museum, Oslo; the School of Mines and the Natural History Museum, Paris; the British Museum (Natural History); the School of Mines, Freiberg, East Germany; and Harvard University.

Nominated by Carl Stentz, Laguna Hills, California
Photographed by Earl Lewis

BROOKITE

Collection: British Museum (Natural History)
Curator: Peter Embrey
Size: 4.6 cm × 3 cm; 1.8″ × 1.2″

Brookite is a rather common titanium mineral, but large, well-formed crystals are very rare. The mineral is of medium hardness, is brittle, is occasionally transparent, and occurs in shades of light-brown to dark-brown and even black. Brookites are most often found in the beautiful alpine regions of Europe. They occur in veins of schist and gneiss and associate with adularia, quartz, albite, anatase, rutile, sphene, muscovite, calcite, and hematite. Crystals of more than one centimeter are rare, but the typical thin tabular shape is commonly reported from numerous localities. Fine crystals have been found at Miask, Ural Mountains, U. S. S. R.; Frossnitz, Tirol, Italy; Abichl-Alp, Salzburg, Austria; Beura, Piedmont, Italy, Graubünden, Switzerland; Bourg d'Oisans, Isère, France; and Magnet Cove, Arkansas. Brookite is named after the English mineralogist, Henry James Brooke (1771–1857).

This specimen of brookite is considered to be one of the finest miniature specimens in the world. The brookite crystal peeks over the top of a water-clear quartz crystal, making for a splendidly matched combination of minerals. This specimen was found in the 1840s at Tremadoc, Caernarvonshire, Wales. A Mr. Wright sold it to the British Museum (Natural History) in 1856. The brookite crystal measures 1″ × 1″; the specimen is number 26967.

Other fine brookites are in the collections of the Bally Museum, Schönenwerd, Switzerland; the Natural History Museum, Bern, Switzerland, and the Swiss Federal Institute of Technology, Zurich; the American Museum of Natural History; the Natural History Museum, Vienna; the National Museum, Prague; and Godehard, Schwethelm, Munich, West Germany.

Nominated by Edward Sopworth, Croydon, England
Photographed by Peter Green and Frank Greenaway

SULFUR

Collection: The Smithsonian Institution
Curator: Paul Desautels
Size: 30.7 cm $\times$ 13.2 cm; 12″ $\times$ 6″

Sulfur is the yellow crystalline element of the mineral world. It occurs in the gases emitted from fumaroles, and frequently forms as the result of volcanic action. In industry it is used in rubber vulcanization and in the making of paper, matches, gunpowder, fireworks, and insecticides. In medicine it is still used in treating skin diseases. Sulfur is obtained as a by-product from a number of minerals, but its most spectacular occurrence is in its native state as bright yellow pyramidal or tabular crystals. Good sulfur crystals require exceptional care since excessive heat or strong light rapidly causes cracks to form, resulting in severe damage to the specimen. Poor handling can produce equally disastrous results. The team of experts inspected hundreds of sulfur crystal groups, many of which undoubtedly were spectacular beauties at one time, but, because of dust, heat, and abrasion, were not of sufficient quality to merit further consideration for this book. The best of the sulfur crystals were mined in Sicily at Agrigento, Cianciana, Rocalmuto, and Cattolica, with the first Sicilian sulfurs being mined as early as A.D. 1250. Other good crystals have come from Pericara, Romagna, Italy; Conil, Cadiz, Spain; and Calcasieu Parish, Louisiana.

This sulfur specimen is very unusual, due to the size and perfection of its crystals and its relative freedom from damage. Mined at Agrigento, Sicily, it was acquired by Mr. E. I. Du Pont de Nemours. The Smithsonian Institution received the specimen by exchange in 1968; it is numbered R16918. The largest crystal is 7.1 cm long (2.7″).

Other fine sulfurs are displayed in the collections of the Institute of Mineralogy and the Civic Museum of Natural Science, both of Milan; the Swiss Federal Institute of Technology, Zurich; the Museum of Natural Science, Madrid; the Natural History Museum, Vienna; and the Institute of Mines, Leningrad.

Photographed by Earl Lewis

TANZANITE

Collection: The Smithsonian Institution
Curator: Paul Desautels
Size: 5.6 cm × 3.3 cm; 2.2″ × 1.3″

As recently as 1967 a beautiful new gemstone was discovered in the upper part of the Umba Valley near the Usumburu Mountains of Tanzania. It was found to be a blue variety of zoisite and was named tanzanite after the country in which it was located. Previously zoisite was known as a pink or a green mineral, but the new tanzanites came in a wide variety of shades ranging from deep-blue to violet. Furthermore, the new stone provided clear sections which produced some of the most beautiful cut stones ever seen. Tanzanite is brilliant and fairly hard, but its most distinguishing feature is its pleochroism: a stone may seem to be a sapphire-blue color when viewed in one direction, and a lavender hue when looked at from another angle. A substantial number of fine tanzanite crystals have been mined in the Umba Valley; blue zoisite has been found nowhere else.

This superb crystal was found in 1969. It was selected because of its color, size, crystal perfection, and clarity (it would produce several excellent cut stones). It was sold to the Smithsonian Institution in 1970 by Martin Ehrmann. It has not yet been catalogued and therefore has no collection number.

Other fine tanzanites are in the collections of Gerhard Becker, Idar-Oberstein, West Germany; Harvard University; the American Museum of Natural History; and Edward Swoboda, Los Angeles.

Photographed by Earl Lewis

ACANTHITE

Collection: British Museum (Natural History)
Curator: Peter Embrey
Size: 13.8 cm × 5.7 cm; 5.6″ × 2.3″

Acanthite is the current name for the black silver-sulfide mineral that previously was called argentite or silver glance. It is usually massive, and as such is the most important primary mineral of silver. One-fourth-inch crystals are unusual, but are seen in most museums. It is the crystal of one-half inch or more that attracts attention, particularly if it is well formed and is upon a good matrix. Acanthite tarnishes easily in strong light, is very heavy, and is so soft that it can be sliced with a knife. Acanthite associates in ore bodies with native silver, proustite, pyrargyrite, pyrite, galena, chalcopyrite, sphalerite, tetrahedrite, calcite, limonite, and quartz. Fine specimens have been found at Kongsberg, Norway; Andreasberg, Harz Mountains, and Annaberg, Saxony, East Germany; Sarrabus, Sardinia, Italy; Liskeard, Cornwall, England; Guanajuato, Mexico; Chañarcillo, Atacama, Chile; Colquechaca, Bolivia; Butte, Montana; and Virginia City, Nevada.

This specimen was mined at the Himmelfahrt Mine at Freiberg, Saxony, in the 1850s. It was sold to the British Museum (Natural History) by Dr. Bondi in 1864. It represents a fine example of the intergrowth of good-sized crystals, the largest of which measures 1.9 cm (.8″), and at least fourteen other crystals are one-half inch in size.

Many of the world's great silver mines have closed, possibly forever, but the fabulous mines of Freiberg, East Germany, are still going strong. Early in the twelfth century silver minerals, associated with ores of bismuth, zinc, cobalt, lead, and nickel, were discovered in the Freiberg veins. Outstanding crystals representing many of these species were found, ignored, and sent to the smelters. Unfortunately, serious and systematic crystal collecting did not exist during those years. While it is true that the very high-grade ore is gone, still there are values of silver remaining, and the supply of lead and zinc ore seems inexhaustible. A bird's-eye view of Freiberg today shows the skyline dotted with the belching stacks of the smelters, the dusty long lines of the mills, and the whirring wheels poised on top of the black mine headframes. Crystals of all sorts of minerals are still arriving (sometimes daily) at the School of Mines offices for identification or for sale. Who knows, possibly tomorrow more bright cubes of acanthite will make their appearance in Freiberg, to the delight of crystal lovers everywhere.

Other choice-quality acanthites are on display in the collections of the American Museum of Natural History; the University of Copenhagen; the School of Mines, Freiberg, East Germany; the Natural History Museum, Paris; the Mining Museum, Kongsberg, Norway; the Smithsonian Institution; the Natural History Museum, Vienna; the Moravian Museum, Brno, Czechoslovakia; and the National Museum, Prague.

Nominated by Thomas Farther, London, England
Photographed by Peter Green and Frank Greenaway

AMAZONSTONE (Amazonite)

Collection: The Smithsonian Institution
Curator: Paul Desautels
Size: 18.2 cm × 17.9 cm; 7.5″ × 7″

Amazonstone is the green or blue-green variety of microcline. Its ingredients are potassium, aluminum, and silicon. It is of average hardness, is usually translucent, and has a bright luster. Amazonstone crystallizes as short, stocky crystals with a perfect cleavage. Good-quality crystals or cleavages are used in ornamental carvings or are cut as cabochons for rings and pendants. Amazonstone resembles and has been erroneously sold as jade. It occasionally associates with smoky quartz, and this combination produces one of the most exotic of all mineral specimens. Amazonstone has been found in the Ilmen Mountains in Central U. S. S. R.; Kragerö, Telemark, and Larvik, Vestfold, in Norway; and at Pikes Peak and Florissant, Teller County, Colorado.

This magnificent specimen was found at Crystal Peak, Teller County, Colorado, in the early 1900s. It was presented to the Smithsonian Institution by Mr. F. W. Clarke, where it became a part of the C. S. Bement Collection on May 4, 1909. The collection number is 86555. There are a half-dozen really fine amazonstone–smoky quartz mineral combinations in existence, but this one was selected because of its crystal perfection, good colors, and striking beauty. It has been used to illustrate articles dealing with minerals many times over the years.

Other fine amazonstone–smoky quartz clusters are in the collections of Harvard University; the American Museum of Natural History; E. M. Gunnell, Denver, Colorado; and the School of Mines, Paris.

Nominated by C. Douglas Woodhouse, Santa Barbara, California
Photographed by Earl Lewis

CALCITE

Collection: British Museum (Natural History)
Curator: Peter Embrey
Size: 18 cm × 12.8 cm; 7″ × 5″

Calcite is one of the most common and widely distributed of all minerals. It occurs as crystals in many different shapes and in almost every conceivable color. Calcite is a soft mineral, is quite brittle, and frequently has a distinct rhombohedral cleavage; when these cleavages are clear, it is called Iceland Spar. These cleavages permit double refraction—that is, a single line viewed through the spar will appear as two lines. Many types fluoresce or phosphoresce when exposed to long or to short ultraviolet waves. Calcite, chemically, is calcium carbonate. Calcite can form as crystals, fibers, scales, sand, and concretions. It readily combines with other minerals, which can and do change its color. It frequently is deposited in thick sedimentary layers from lime-bearing waters. It is commonly associated with quartz, fluorite, siderite, dolomite, barite, galena, and sphalerite. Fine crystals of calcite have been found at Helgustadir, Eskifjördur, Iceland (the largest measured 20′ × 6.5′); Chalanches, Allemont, France; Rhisnes, Belgium; Přibram, Bohemia, Czechoslovakia; Weardale, Lancashire, England; Andreasberg, Harz Mountains, East Germany; Kongsberg, Norway; Hamman Meskoutine, Gudma, Algeria; Guanajuato, Mexico; Joplin, Missouri; Bisbee, Arizona; and Ottawa County, Quebec, Canada.

This specimen was selected over hundreds of spectacular calcite crystals because of the perfection, color, and jackstraw shape of the crystal group. It was mined in the early 1900s at Bigrigg, Cumberland, England, and was first purchased by Mr. J. Graves of Frizington, Cumberland, England, who presented it to the British Museum (Natural History) in 1903. It was used as Figure 6, Plate III, in A. L. Tutton's book *Crystals,* published in 1911. Its longest crystal is 15.4 (6″) long. Its number in the museum is 86419.

Other fine calcites are in the collections of the Faculty of Sciences and the School of Mines, Paris; Arlis Coger, Huntsville, Arkansas; the Geological Museum, London; and the Cranbrook Institute of Science, Bloomfield Hills, Michigan.

Nominated by A. M. Wali, London, England
Photographed by Peter Green and Frank Greenaway

ROSE QUARTZ

Collection: H. Rudolf Becker, Idar-Oberstein, West Germany
Size: 17.5 cm × 10.2 cm; 7″ × 4.1″

Rose quartz is relatively hard, frequently has a pleasing rich rose-pink color, and occasionally is free enough of imperfections to be used in carvings and cabochon stones. Rose quartz usually occurs in the central quartz core of pegmatite veins. Until a few years ago good-quality rose quartz crystals were unknown, due to the fact that in the ore body rose quartz tends to fill the cavity completely, leaving no room for crystal growth. Beginning in early 1959, small clusters of rose quartz crystals were brought into the Brazilian upcountry towns of Pedra Azul, Teofilo Otoni, and Governador Valadares. At first skeptics evaluated these stones as artificially colored white quartz crystals. Others said that even if these were genuine rose quartz crystals, they would rapidly bleach and lose their color in the sunlight. Nevertheless, this new find created considerable interest in the mineral world. In the next few months new discoveries brought to light large groups of rose quartz crystals so spectacular as to rank with the most beautiful specimens of any mineral ever before found. The colors were proved to be natural and did not fade in ordinary light.

This extraordinary example of rose quartz was selected for its exceptional beauty. Its crystals have grown artistically about the larger whitish quartz crystals, and nature has added a dusting of brownish eosphorite crystals for good measure. It was found in the Arassuahy-Jequitinhonha mining district, Minas Gerais, Brazil, in 1971.

Other important rose quartz crystal groups are in the collections of the Smithsonian Institution; the Geological Museum, London; and Peter Bancroft, Ramona, California.

Nominated by Gerhard Becker, Idar-Oberstein, West Germany
Photographed by Karl Hartmann

LEGRANDITE

Collection: The Smithsonian Institution
Curator: Paul Desautels
Size: 22.8 cm × 15.6 cm; 9.3" × 6.2"

Legrandite is one of the rarest, most beautiful minerals known. It was first discovered by a Mr. Legrand, a Belgian mine manager, in the 1920s. The locality was a zinc mine named the Flor de Pena near Lampazas, Nuevo León, Mexico; this is the only mine that has produced legrandite. Only a few good-quality legrandite specimens made their way out of Mexico over the years, until new pockets were discovered in 1968. Since that time a few hundred legrandites have been offered for sale and have found homes throughout the world. Legrandite contains zinc and arsenic and occurs as radiating yellow-to-orange crystals. Most legrandite crystals form in small vugs of the iron oxide mineral limonite. It is also found with sphalerite, pyrite, and siderite.

Other fine legrandites are in the collections of the American Museum of Natural History; Edward Bancroft, San Diego, California; and Thomas McKee, Paradise Valley, Arizona.

This specimen was discovered in 1968 and possesses the largest known terminated crystals. The biggest crystal is 3.1 cm × 1.3 cm (1.25" × .4"). The Smithsonian Institution bought it from Mr. Benny J. Fenn on April 16, 1969. It was purchased with Roebling funds and is now a part of the Roebling Collection. The collection number is R17300. Approximately one-half of the specimen is shown.

Nominated by Thomas McKee, Paradise Valley, Arizona
Photographed by Earl Lewis

PEROVSKITE

Collection: British Museum (Natural History)
Curator: Peter Embrey
Size: 11.4 cm × 8.9 cm; 4.5″ × 3.5″

Perovskite is a rare mineral which contains some common elements, calcium and titanium, and which sometimes includes much rarer elements—cerium, erbium, yttrium, and lanthanum. The mineral forms in brown or black roughly shaped cubic crystals which occur in metamorphosed limestones and schists and in basic pegmatites. Perovskite is of average hardness and weight and usually has a brilliant appearance. It is too rare to be used commercially, but good crystals are highly prized by the collector. It was discovered in chlorite schist in the Ural Mountains of the U. S. S. R. and has since been obtained from Schelingen, Kaiserstuhl, Baden, West Germany; Oberweisenthal, Saxony, East Germany; Eifel, West Germany; St. Ambrogio, Piedmont, Italy; Emerese, Val d'Aosta, Italy; Catalao Goyaz, Minas Gerais, Brazil; and Norrvik, Sweden. Perovskite was named after Count L. A. Perovski of St. Petersburg (Leningrad).

This specimen was obtained by the British Museum (Natural History) in 1865 from Mr. Kokscharow, who brought substantial collections of minerals to England from Russia. It was found at Achmatovsk near Kussinsk in the Zlatoust district of the Ural Mountains. The matrix is blue calcite. The largest crystal measures 3.3 cm (1.3″). Its collection number is 39111.

Other fine perovskite specimens are on display at the Institute of Mines, Leningrad; the School of Mines, Paris; and the Institute of Mineralogy, Turin. A magnificent matrix is in the Fersman Mineralogical Museum, Moscow.

Nominated by Alan Jobbins, Geological Museum, London
Photographed by Peter Green and Frank Greenaway

ANHYDRITE

Collection: American Museum of Natural History
Curator: Vincent Manson
Size: 5.7 cm × 4.4 cm; 2.25″ × 1.75″

Anhydrite is a mineral which after refining is used as a soil conditioner, a retarder of the setting action of portland cement, and as an agent in the manufacture of sulfuric acid. It is a very common mineral and is found in huge deposits in many parts of the world.

Such an introduction may cause one to ponder, "Why was anhydrite placed in the Gallery of this book?" Inclusion was made simply because top-quality anhydrite crystals are some of the most prized specimens in any collection.

The crystal shown here is the best-known example of the gem lavender variety of anhydrite. Such fine crystals are extremely rare and have been collected at Salzburg, Austria; and Stassfurt, East Germany. Lesser anhydrite crystals have been found at a salt mine northeast of Bex, and at Granges and Leissigen, all in Switzerland.

This specimen was found in the Simplon Tunnel of Switzerland while it was being cut during the 1920s; the tunnel, which connects southern Switzerland with northern Italy, is nearly seventeen miles long. The best of the anhydrite crystals were found in gypsum and anhydrite clefts about 9500 meters from the north entrance.

As the mineral collector speeds through the tunnel deep beneath the Swiss Alps, he must know that behind the cemented walls, at a point 9500 meters from the Brig entrance, other choice lavender anhydrite crystals lie forever sealed from his prospecting pick. During the days of construction, the tunnel schedule simply didn't allow time to recover all crystals in the area. Only those in the path of the bore itself were saved. This specimen is rated the largest and darkest-colored completely flawless block of anhydrite in existence. Its collection number is 36899.

Other fine anhydrites are in the collections of Godehard Schwethelm, Munich, West Germany; the Faculty of Sciences, Paris; the British Museum (Natural History); and the Natural History Museum, Basel, Switzerland.

Nominated by Eric B. Rubenstein, Flushing, New York
Photographed by Arthur Singer, New York City

CASSITERITE

Collection: The Smithsonian Institution
Curator: Paul Desautels
Size: 15 cm × 11.3 cm; 6″ × 4.5″

Cassiterite is the most important ore of tin. It is also known as tinstone and tin ore. Cassiterite is commonly brown or black, but is found infrequently in other colors, such as white, gray, yellow, or red. It is a heavy mineral and is fairly hard. It forms in extremely brilliant, short, prismatic crystals. Crystals are not uncommon, but they become "unusual" at half an inch and "rare" at one inch. Cassiterite is characteristically a high-temperature mineral and forms in veins or large sumps. It associates with wolframite, quartz, fluorite, bismuthinite, molybdenite, and tourmaline.

Tin is used for protective metal coatings, soft solders, and alloys. Cassiterite was named after the Greek word for "tin." Tin mines are notorious for being located in the nearly inaccessible reaches of high mountains. Most of the Bolivian tin mines are at elevations above 13,000 feet.

Fine cassiterite crystals have been found at Schlaggenwald, Bohemia, Czechoslovakia; St. Christoph, Breitenbrunn, Saxony, East Germany; Villeder, Morbihan, France; Emmaville, Glen Innes, New South Wales, Australia; Siglo Vente Mine, Catavi; Potosi; and Llallagua, all in Bolivia; and the Colcoath lode, Redruth, Cornwall, England. It was from this mine and tin mines in the area that Julius Caesar obtained tin for his Roman Empire.

This specimen contains the largest and finest cassiterite crystals known. It was found in the 1930s at the Fazenda do Funil, Ponto do Reis, Ferros, Minas Gerais, Brazil. The Smithsonian Institution purchased it from Mr. Allan Caplan in 1940, with Canfield funds; it now is part of the Canfield Collection and has the collection number C5698.

Other fine cassiterites are in the collections of Mrs. Mark Bandy, Salt Lake City, Utah; the Natural History Museum, Paris; the British Museum (Natural History); the Fersman Mineralogical Museum, Moscow; Harvard University; the School of Mines, Freiberg, East Germany; the Natural History Museum, Vienna; the Museum of Natural History, Oporto University, Oporto, Portugal; and the National Museum, Prague.

Nominated by Charles Key, St. Petersburg, Florida
Photographed by Earl Lewis

138

CROCOITE

Collection: Edward Swoboda, Los Angeles
Size: 11 cm × 4.5 cm; 4.3″ × 1.8″

Nearly all of the world's supply of choice crystallized crocoite comes from the Australian island of Tasmania, and most of these crocoites were mined many years ago. Crocoite is a bright orange lead-chromate mineral with long, prismatic crystals. Frequently the terminations are broken in removing the specimens from the mine. Nevertheless, the brilliant and vivid slender crystals are a prize in any collection. Crocoite occurs only rarely. It usually forms in hot solutions within oxidized lead deposits as a secondary mineral. Good crystals have come from Sverdlovsk (formerly Ekaterinburg), where it was first found, and in Mursinsk, both in the Ural Mountains of the U. S. S. R.; Rezbanya, Rumania; Goyabeira, Congonhas do Campo, Minas Gerais, Brazil; Penchalonga mine, Umtali, Rhodesia; and Dundas, Tasmania, Australia. Crocoite associates with cerussite, chrome cerussite, wulfenite, limonite, pyromorphite, vanadinite, and descloizite.

This specimen was found in the Adelaide mine, Dundas, in the 1920s. The nearby town of Zeehan is today's gathering place for the area's miners, who wait patiently for better days. Zeehan is really all that remains of the once-boisterous mining camp of Dundas. Dundas is gone and most of the lead mines are flooded, caved in, or closed. Only infrequently does a good crocoite appear, attesting to the efforts of high graders. Zeehan centers about the century-old Central Hotel; many of its shops and the music hall are now closed, but the Zeehan Mining Museum is well worth the trip to this out-of-the-way old town. The museum houses eight or ten magnificent and large crocoite specimens.

Other fine crocoites are in the collections of the Australian Museum, Sydney; Albert Chapman, Sydney; the British Museum (Natural History); the School of Mines, Freiberg, East Germany; the Natural History Museum, Vienna; the School of Mines, Madrid; the Faculty of Sciences and the Natural History Museum, Paris; the Faculty of Sciences, Lisbon; the Royal Museum of Natural History, Stockholm; the American Museum of Natural History; and Peter Bancroft, Ramona, California.

Nominated by Robert Ramsey, San Diego, California
Photographed by Earl Lewis

PROUSTITE

Collection: British Museum (Natural History)
Curator: Peter Embrey
Size: 8.3 cm × 6.4 cm; 3.3″ × 2.5″

One of the most vivid colors in all mineraldom is the scarlet-vermilion of proustite. Occasionally proustite forms in nearly transparent prismatic crystals; it is then that the color of the mineral strikingly resembles that of the ruby. Unfortunately, proustite is soft and easily tarnishes, thus ruling out the possibility of its being used as a commercial gemstone. Proustite is one of the ruby silver minerals found in most silver deposits. It forms in low-temperature formations and occurs late in primary mineral deposition. The better crystals are usually found in pockets (vugs) in the upper levels of silver ore bodies. Excellent crystals have been found at Batopilas, Chihuahua, Mexico; the Himmelfürst mine, Freiberg, East Germany; Ste. Marie aux Mines, Alsace, France; Sarrabus, Sardinia, Italy; Joachimsthal, Bohemia, Czechoslovakia; and the Keeley Mine, South Lorrain, Cobalt, Ontario, Canada. Exceptional proustites are a rarity, and, because of the tarnishing factor, fine crystals stored away from sunlight or even artificial light are therefore seldom seen in mineral displays. Proustite was named after the French chemist J. L. Proust (1754–1826).

This specimen was mined at Chañarcillo, Atacama, Chile, in about 1895; over the years this locality has produced most of the great proustites. It was purchased by the British Museum (Natural History) from a Mr. R. Jacques in 1900. At that time it was regarded as the "largest known proustite crystal." Today, although there are larger crystals in some collections, this specimen was judged superior because of its size, crystal perfection, and magnificent color. Its collection number is 84698.

Other fine proustites are in the collections of John Jago, San Francisco; the School of Mines, Mexico City; the School of Mines, Paris; the Smithsonian Institution; the American Museum of Natural History; the Geology Museum, Oslo; the School of Mines, Freiberg, East Germany; the National Museum, Prague; and the University of Chile, Santiago.

Nominated by C. Douglas Woodhouse, Santa Barbara, California
Photographed by Peter Green and Frank Greenaway

LUDLOCKITE

Collection: David Wilber, Reno, Nevada
Size: 4.5 cm × 3.8 cm; 1.8″ × 1.5″

One of the most unusual and perhaps least known of the minerals in the Gallery is ludlockite. But for a combined stroke of luck and wisdom on the part of Frederick Smith, a New Jersey mineral dealer, the mineral might still be unknown. In 1967, while Mr. Smith was on a mineral-buying trip in Tsumeb, South-West Africa, one evening he dropped by a miner's house to inquire if by chance he had any minerals for sale. During the visit Mr. Smith noticed a twelve-inch chunk of what he believed to be germanium ore on the front porch. Little vugs of tiny brownish crystals on the outside of the rock made him curious as to whether better crystals existed within. Fortunately the miner was cooperative. The piece was split open, and, to the delight of those present, a six-inch cavity filled with bright brownish crystals was exposed. Mr. Smith bought the crystals and transported them to the United States, where they proved to be crystals of a brand-new mineral. Mr. Smith's full name is Frederick *Lud*low Smith, III, and his partner's name is Charles *Lock*e Key; the mineral was named after the middle names of the two men—ludlockite. Only a handful of ludlockite specimens exist; to date the only source has been the rock at the miner's house in Tsumeb.

This specimen is by far the largest and best of the ludlockites. Dealers, curators, and collectors alike acclaim it to be one of the most exciting new specimens to be discovered during the last decade. Just as the Mona Lisa is not the largest of the paintings, this bit of crystal beauty has real quality among all minerals. Ludlockite is composed of iron and arsenic. Other ludlockites are in the collections of Edward Swoboda, Los Angeles, and William Larson, Fallbrook, California.

Nominated by George Holloway, Northridge, California
Photographed by Earl Lewis

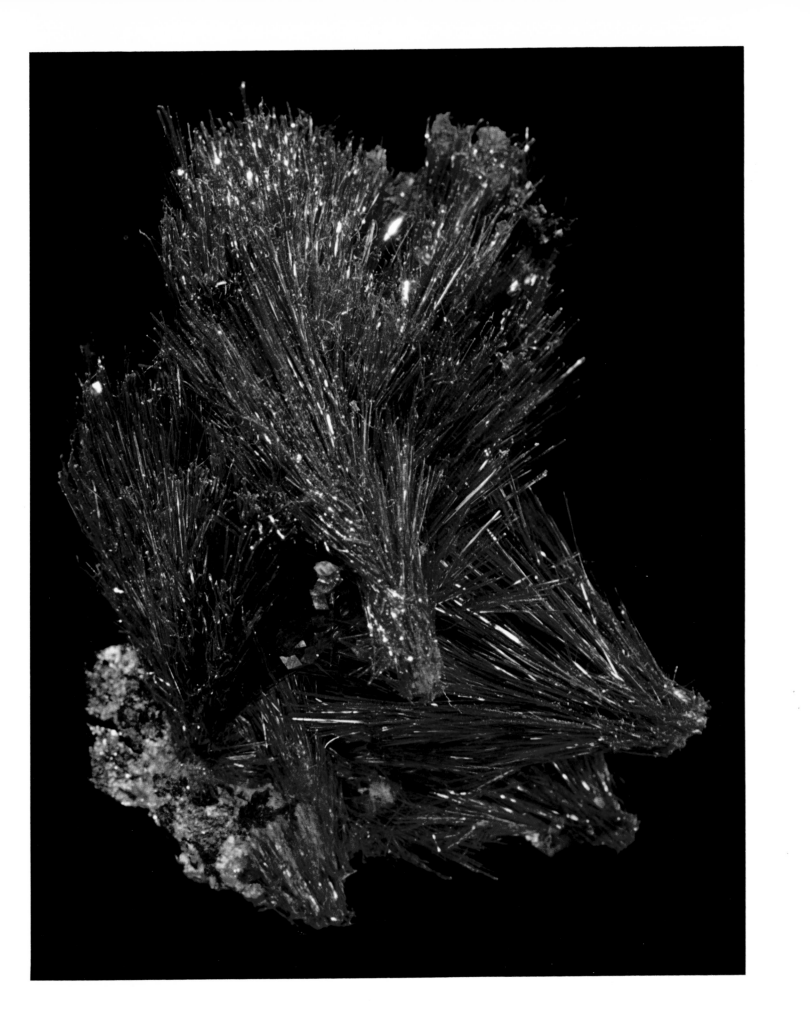

BLUE TOPAZ

Collection: Fersman Mineralogical Museum, Moscow
Director: G. P. Barsanov
Secretary: Orlov Leonidovich
Size: 12.7 cm × 10.2 cm; 5″ × 4″

Crystallized blue topaz is one of the most beautiful and classic of all gem crystals. It has a soft baby-blue color, is hard, and is reasonably brilliant. Blue topaz is popular as a moderately priced gemstone. It is found in the Ural Mountains and in the Ukraine in the U. S. S. R.; the Mourne Mountains, County Down, Ireland; various localities in Minas Gerais, Brazil; Miami, Rhodesia; and Ramona, California.

This superb crystal was mined in the Ural Mountains at Alabaschka, near Mursinsk, Sverdlovsk, U. S. S. R., in about 1850. It is part of the magnificent mineral and gem collection of the Fersman Mineralogical Museum of the U. S. S. R. Academy of Sciences. The collection began when Peter the Great, in 1716, ordered the Danzig Collection of 1195 specimens to be purchased. This initial collection was to become the start of the Academy of Sciences mineralogy section. With the years, the collection grew, in both depth and quality, and in 1934 it was permanently housed in the former "riding-house" of Count A. G. Orlov. The museum was named the Fersman Mineralogical Museum after the museum's early academician, A. Y. Fersman, an outstanding Russian mineralogist. Today the museum is a scientific repository containing 120,000 samples of minerals, a number of them unique in size. It also houses a priceless collection of decorative and precious stones. The collection includes a giant blue topaz crystal (7″ × 12″) and a wall case filled with well-formed blue crystals of topaz, many of them in matrixes of smoky quartz crystals, feldspar, and mica.

Other fine blue topazes are in the collections of the Mining Institute Museum, Leningrad; the School of Mines, Paris; the British Museum (Natural History); Harvard University; the Field Museum, Chicago; the American Museum of Natural History; and the Smithsonian Institution.

Photographed by E. Cogan, Moscow

SPERRYLITE

Collection: British Museum (Natural History)
Curator: Peter Embrey
Size: 6.2 cm × 5.1 cm; 2.9″ × 2.5″

Sperrylite is one of only three minerals which contain any of the rare metal platinum. Sperrylite is a very heavy mineral, fairly hard, and tin-white in color. Its crystals form as cubes but sometimes change to octahedrons with very rounded corners and edges. Nearly all crystals are small. Sperrylite contains, in addition to platinum, small amounts of arsenic, rhodium, antimony, iron, and copper. It was first discovered at the Vermilion mine, Algoma District, twenty-two miles west of Sudbury, Ontario, Canada. It has since been found at Nikolaevsky, Amur, eastern Siberia, U. S. S. R.; in the Rambler Mine, Medicine Bow Mountains, Wyoming; and in the Little Tennessee River, Franklin, Macon County, North Carolina.

This specimen contains the world's largest and best-formed crystal of sperrylite, measuring 2.4 cm × 1.9 cm (.83″ × .75″). The matrix is limonite, a common iron mineral. It was found on the Tweefontein farm, ten miles northwest of Potgietersrust, Waterberg District, Transvaal, South Africa, about 1924. It was received from the Chairman of the Potgietersrust Platinum Mining Company and presented to the British Museum (Natural History) by George H. Beatty, Esq., of Johannesburg, Transvaal, South Africa, on July 12, 1926. It was described in *Mining Magazine,* 1926, volume 21, page 96. Its collection number is 1926–445.

Sperrylite was named after Francis Sperry, who recognized it as a new mineral. Sperry was a chemist from Sudbury.

Other sperrylite specimens are in the collections of the Smithsonian Institution; the Manchester University Museum, Manchester, England; and the Institute of Mineralogy, Heidelberg, West Germany. Smaller crystals of fine quality have been reported to be in a museum at either Capetown or Durban, South Africa.

Nominated by Charles Key, St. Petersburg, Florida
Photographed by Peter Green and Frank Greenaway

AMETHYST

Collection: Gerhard Becker, Idar-Oberstein, West Germany
Size: 30.5 cm × 22.9 cm; 12″ × 9″

Amethyst is the lavender-colored member of the quartz family. Since a tiny amount of iron is always present in an amethyst crystal, it is believed that this element is the coloring agent. Amethyst was well-known to the ancients and has been found in the jewelry of the early Egyptians. It was usually set as cabochons or as natural crystals. The combined resources of today's cutting shops produce thousands of carats of faceted amethyst daily. Light shades are common and quite inexpensive. Dark clear stones are highly prized and therefore more costly, although as gemstones, amethyst of any quality is comparatively inexpensive.

Amethyst crystals which line the pockets or vugs of quartz veins most frequently are removed singly from the pocket in order to assure less damage to the gem sections. Occasionally, however, the whole vug may be removed intact. Sometimes amethyst crystals are so small as to form a lavender druse upon other crystals, but some individual prisms are known to have weighed fifty pounds or more.

Good-quality amethyst crystals have been found at Zillertal, Tyrol, Austria; Schemnitz, Czechoslovakia; Pokura, Transylvania, Rumania; Mursinsk, Sverdlovsk, U. S. S. R.; Madras, India; Artigas, Uruguay; Rio Grande do Sul, Brazil; Amherst, Virginia; and Alexander County, North Carolina.

This specimen was mined at Guanajuato, Mexico, in about 1960. It was selected from hundreds of fine amethyst crystal groups, many of them quite gemmy, because of the size of the crystals, the rich color at the crystal tips, and the crystal arrangement of the cluster.

Other fine amethysts are in the collections of Geological Museum, London; the School of Mines and the Faculty of Sciences, both of Paris; the School of Mines, Freiberg, East Germany; the American Museum of Natural History; and Manuel Ontiveros, El Paso, Texas.

Photographed by Karl Hartmann

STOLZITE

Collection: The Smithsonian Institution
Curator: Paul Desautels
Size: 11.4 cm × 6.3 cm; 4.4″ × 2.5″

Stolzite is a rather rare mineral which infrequently crystallizes. Because its elements are lead and tungsten, it is occasionally mistaken for another rare lead tungstate mineral, raspite. Stolzite is soft, brittle, and resembles wulfenite in crystal form, but is somewhat heavier. It occurs in various colors, including red, green, yellow, and brown. Stolzite is avidly sought by the advanced collector, and the mere mention of its name has caused many a mineral fancier to travel considerable distances in an effort to obtain a good specimen. It is found at Zinnwald, Bohemia, Czechoslovakia; Bleiberg, Carinthia, Austria; Berggiesshübel, Saxony, East Germany; the Force Craig lead mine, Keswick, Cumberland, England; Abuja, northern Nigeria; Marianna de Itacolumy, Ouro Prêto, Minas Gerais, Brazil; the Huachuca Mountains, south of Tombstone, Arizona; the Prismos mine, Dragoon, Arizona; the Grouse Creek Mountains, Lucin, Utah; the Wheatley lead mine, Chester County, Pennsylvania; and the Cariboo Mountains, British Columbia, Canada.

This specimen was found at the Proprietary Mine, Broken Hill, New South Wales, Australia, in the 1920s. It was presented to the Smithsonian Institution in 1963. Its collection number is 116912.

Other fine stolzites are in the collections of the British Museum (Natural History); the School of Mines, Freiberg, East Germany; the Faculty of Sciences and the School of Mines, both of Paris; the National Museum, Prague; and the Australian Museum.

Photographed by Earl Lewis

NATIVE GOLD

Collection: Cranbrook Institute of Science, Bloomfield Hills, Michigan
Director: Warren L. Wittry
Size: 26 cm × 14.1 cm; 10.1″ × 5.5″

Gold has been coveted throughout history as a beautiful, rare, and consequently valuable mineral. Gold is widely distributed over the earth and is found in the sands and gravels of the valleys of auriferous regions, in quartz veins and seams, in sedimentary rocks, frequently in metamorphic rocks, and even in sea water. Some gold samples contain small percentages of copper, silver, palladium, or bismuth. Gold which contains a high percentage of silver is known as argentiferous gold or electrum. The ancient Egyptians displayed two obelisks of solid electrum before their temples in Thebes. The Assyrian king, who sacked Thebes during the reign of Tanoutamun, took the obelisks as prizes of war, and listed them as weighing 2500 talents (83 tons). The electrum alloy was composed of 75 per cent gold, 22 per cent silver, and 3 per cent copper.

Fine gold specimens have been found at Hill End, New South Wales, Australia (wire masses weighing more than two hundred pounds); Johannesburg, Transvaal, South Africa; Magdalena, Sonora, Mexico; the Bunker Hill Mine, Amador City, California; Carson Hill, Calaveras County, California (a nugget found in 1854 weighed 147 pounds); and the extremely rich region on the east slope of the Ural Mountains, U. S. S. R.

This superb specimen was selected for its size, brilliance, and pleasing form. It was found at the Red Ledge Mines, Washington, Nevada County, California. It is formed of an aggregate of "leaves" and crystals of nearly pure gold. It was mined in 1914 in the winze of the south drift at the two-hundred-foot level. The Red Ledge Mines are at a site discovered between the years 1897 and 1907. This mine has produced a substantial number of outstanding gold specimens, some of them crystals. Many fine pieces were found nearly at the surface, covered with mud and occasionally intertwined with bush and tree roots. In later years Sam P. Tracy became a part owner of the Red Ledge. More recently this ownership passed to his wife, Mrs. Stella Tracy. This mine is inactive now and is closed to the public.

Other fine gold specimens are in the collections of the New Library Museum, Johannesburg, South Africa; Harvard University; the Smithsonian Institution; the Colorado State Museum, Denver; C. Douglas Woodhouse, Santa Barbara, California; and the California State Mining Bureau, San Francisco.

Nominated by Stella Tracy, Washington, California
Photographed by Earl Lewis

GROSSULAR

Collection: Carla Larson, Fallbrook, California
Size: 5 cm × 3.2 cm; 2″ × 1.25″

Grossular is one species in the garnet series. It is fairly hard, and when found in clear crystals will cut into beautiful faceted stones. "Grossular" comes from "Grossularia," the botanical name for gooseberry. Grossular occurs in various shades of pink, orange, yellow, brown, and green. Other names for grossular are cinnamon-stone, essonite, hessonite, hyacinth, South African jade, Transvaal jade, and rosolite. It crystallizes into twelve-sided shapes (dodecahedrons) which are usually bright and amazingly well formed. Grossular is most frequently found in metamorphosed limestone. It associates with vesuvianite, diopside, scapolite, tourmaline, and wollastonite. Good crystals have been found at Xalostoc, Morelos, Mexico; Monzoni and Trentino, Piedmont, Italy; the island of Elba, Italy; Zermatt, Valais, Switzerland; the Vilyui River, Yakutsk, U. S. S. R.; Ramona, California; Oravita and Dognacska, Rumania; Achmatovsk, Kussinsk, U. S. S. R.; and Asbestos, Quebec, Canada.

This pert little specimen displays a crown of extremely rich-colored grossular crystals perched on top of a diopside crystal. This matrix was mined in 1950 at Eden Mills, Vermont, and is one of three known fine specimens from this location.

Other choice grossulars are in the collections of David Wilber, Reno, Nevada; Edward Swoboda, Los Angeles; William Sanborn, Newport Beach, California; the Natural History Museum, Vienna; University of Milan, Institute of Mineralogy Museum; the School of Mines, Paris; the Institute of Mineralogy, Rome; the Institute of Mineralogy, Turin; the Moravian Museum, Brno, Czechoslovakia; the Institute of Chemical Technology, Prague; Harvard University; Alfred Buranek, Salt Lake City, Utah; Charles Key, St. Petersburg, Florida; and the National Museum of Natural Sciences, Ottawa, Canada.

Nominated by Edward Swoboda, Los Angeles
Photographed by Earl Lewis

EMERALD

Collection: American Museum of Natural History
Curator: Vincent Manson
Size: 6.6 cm × 3.1 cm; 2.6″ × 1.2″

Emerald is the blue-green to grass-green variety of beryl. The beryl family also includes aquamarine (blue), morganite (pink), and golden beryl (yellow). Emerald tends to flaw in nature, and it is a rare crystal that is without cracks. The deep, rich green color is most prized. Very large crystals are nearly always full of flaws. An emerald is worth almost four times as much as a diamond of equal size and quality. Even though synthetic emeralds are common, the true emerald remains one of the most treasured of all gemstones. Fine emeralds of great size (1″ × 2″ or larger) have commanded prices in excess of one million dollars.

This emerald has been named the Patricia and was selected for its crystal perfection, size, and superb color. Seldom is a giant emerald so well-formed. It is heavily flawed, but this rather normal tendency of the emerald does not prevent this crystal from being one of the world's great gem crystals. It was found in 1966 in the Chivor emerald mine, located about 130 kilometers northwest of the Colombian capital city of Bogotá. This mine was established by the Chibcha Indians during the fifteenth century. The Spanish conquistadores captured the mine in 1537 and worked it for the next 150 years. The mine is operating today and is still producing a steady supply of magnificent gem emeralds.

Emeralds were first mined thousands of years ago. As early as 2000 B.C. the Egyptians mined emeralds at Gebel Zabara on the Upper Nile. Some of these stones, mounted in pendant and pectoral jewelry, may be seen today in the Cairo Museum. Emeralds were discovered near Sverdlovsk in Russia's Ural Mountains about 1830. Other emerald localities are Habachtal, Salzburg, Austria; Muzo, Colombia; the Transvaal, South Africa; and Stony Point, North Carolina.

Other fine emeralds are in the collections of the School of Mines, Paris; and the Natural History Museum, Vienna.

Nominated by Charles Key, St. Petersburg, Florida
Photographed by Arthur Singer

RHODOCHROSITE

Collection: Peter Bancroft, Ramona, California
Size: 14 cm × 12 cm; 5.5″ × 4.7″

Rhodochrosite, in its rose-pink to ruby-red colors, is one of the loveliest minerals to grace any collection. In addition, it frequently associates with quartz, pyrite, and calcite in pleasing combinations. Rhodochrosite is a manganese carbonate. It is soft and has a strong cleavage, rendering it inadequate for cut stones. Its crystals are often bright and form as perfect rhombohedrons, with half-inch crystals somewhat common and two-inch crystals being exceptionally rare. Pink rhodochrosite comes from a number of localities, including Capillitas, Catamarca, Argentina; Ljubija district, Yugoslavia; Moët-Fontaine, Ardennes, Belgium; Siegen, Westphalia, West Germany; Mazul, Krasnoyarsk, Siberia, U. S. S. R.; Vielle Aure, Hautes-Pyrénées, France; Butte, Montana; Park City, Utah; and the John Reed mine, Alicante, Lake County, Colorado. Rhodochrosite occurs in fairly low-temperature veins of silver, zinc, and lead mines. The material found in Capillitas, Argentina, occurs as botryoidal banded pink masses which when curved or slabbed and polished produce beautiful display pieces. It is mined commercially at Butte, Montana, where veins are very large, to be used as a drier in paints, as a component in the manufacture of chlorine and bromine, and as a decolorizer in glass.

This remarkable specimen was found at Alma, Park County, Colorado, a locality which over the years has produced the best rhodochrosites in the world. It was found by a miner who, feeling that more rhodochrosite crystals still remained in the extremely hard quartz veins located high in the Rocky Mountains, in 1965 drove a 120-foot tunnel from the back of the mine and located a pocket which produced the richest-colored rhodochrosite crystals ever found. The story is told that the miner sold the crystals for a substantial amount of money and then frittered his profits away within a few weeks in a series of "happy times" at a local saloon.

This specimen is the best one found by that miner. One section of the four-inch ruby-red crystal is transparent. The white crystals are quartz, the yellow are iron pyrite, and the black are tetrahedrite.

Other fine rhodochrosites from Alma are to be seen in the collections of the School of Mines, Paris; the Royal Museum of Natural History, Stockholm; the Natural History Museum, Fribourg, Switzerland; the Smithsonian Institution; the Morgan Collection of the American Museum of Natural History; David Wilber, Reno, Nevada; and the Humboldt University, Berlin.

Nominated by Glen Frost, La Jolla, California
Photographed by Earl Lewis

KUNZITE

Collection: The Smithsonian Institution
Curator: Paul Desautels
Size: 31 cm × 15.3 cm; 12.1″ × 6″

Kunzite is the lovely lilac-colored variety of spodumene. It was first discovered in the Pala Chief mine at Pala, California, in 1903. A Mr. Baskerville named it kunzite in honor of G. F. Kunz, an early-day American gem expert. Kunzite crystals are strongly dichroic, in that the intensity of color varies with the angle or direction of the light as it passes through the stone. Kunzites are fairly hard but are difficult to cut, due to a strong prismatic cleavage. Kunzite occurs in pegmatite veins where lithia is present. It commonly associates with lithia mica, lepidolite, and lithia tourmaline. Many crystals etch from mineral solutions while still in the ground, leaving only a few with clean crystal faces. Kunzite is fashioned by the lapidist into beautiful pink stones with step, oval, or round cuts. This gemstone "twins": a single crystal may resemble two crystals that have grown together along a prism face. Kunzite crystals have been found at the Victor mine, Rincon, California; in the state of Minas Gerais, Brazil; and on the island of Madagascar.

This magnificent kunzite crystal weighs 7.5 kilos (16.5 pounds) and has no broken surfaces on its crystal faces. It is a fine example of a "twinned" crystal. The stone is virtually without flaw and of the finest color—a deep greenish color in one direction and a rich purple in another. It is considered the largest and best kunzite crystal in existence. It was found in the Urucupa mine at Itambacuri, Minas Gerais, Brazil, in 1961. It was acquired by Paulo Nercessian of Rio de Janeiro, who sold it to Martin Ehrmann, who in 1962 sent it to the Smithsonian Institution as part of an exchange.

Other large and very beautiful kunzite crystals are on display at the American Museum of Natural History; the School of Mines and the Natural History Museum, Paris; and Harvard University.

Photographed by Earl Lewis

ERYTHRITE

Collection: School of Mines, Paris
Curator: Claude Guillemin
Size: 16 cm × 11 cm; 6.4″ × 4.4″

Erythrite combines the elements of cobalt, nickel, and arsenic, and is therefore a basic ore of cobalt and nickel. Crystals are soft and occur in dense, very hard ores, making recovery of undamaged crystals most difficult. In addition, erythrite crystals occur rarely, so good specimens are in great demand. Erythrite crystals vary in color from crimson red to apple green. The better crystals come from Timiskaming, Ontario, Canada; Schneeberg, Saxony, East Germany; Příbram, Bohemia, Czechoslovakia; the Turtmannthal, Valais, Switzerland; and Leogang, Salzburg, Austria.

This erythrite specimen was found at the relatively new locality of Bou Azzer, Morocco, in 1957. It was obtained by the French Geological Mission to Morocco in 1959. The largest crystal is 1.5 cm or .6″ long. Morocco has been a heavy producer of top-quality minerals during the past fifteen years. In addition to erythrite, Moroccan quality minerals are vanadinite, mimetite, and other lead minerals.

Other fine erythrite specimens are displayed in the collections of David Wilber, Reno, Nevada; the School of Mines, Freiberg, East Germany; and the Faculty of Sciences, Paris.

Nominated by H. J. Schubnel, Paris
Photographed by Jacques Six

SIDERITE (Pseudomorph after Fluorite)

Collection: British Museum (Natural History)
Curator: Peter Embrey
Size: 10.2 cm × 8.75 cm; 4″ × 3.5″

This siderite cube is one of the most unusual mineral specimens ever discovered. Originally this mineral was a fluorite crystal of green or blue color, resting in an ore pocket deep in an English lead mine. Over many years thermal solutions slowly ate away the fluorite and replaced a part of the crystal with a new mineral—the iron carbonate siderite. The siderite retained the form of the fluorite but none of the fluorine mineral remained. This pseudomorphosis also left the crystal hollow, and, later in the crystal's history, additional heated vapors bearing iron and silica deposited other minerals within the cavity. First grew the brass-colored chalcopyrite, to be followed by the white spires of quartz; remarkably enough, the outer structure of siderite was undamaged during the transformation.

This specimen was found in the Virtuous Lady Mine at Tavistock, Devonshire, England, in 1846. Its first owner, E. Pearse, sold it to the British Museum (Natural History) in 1847. It is currently on display just inside the entrance of the Mineral Gallery of the British Museum, and is listed as "chalybite," a rather common name in Europe for siderite. Its collection number is BM 21338.

Photographed by Peter Green and Frank Greenaway

BRAZILIANITE

Collection: Paul Fraenkel, Paris
Size: 8.1 cm × 3.2 cm; 3.2″ × 1.3″

Brazilianite is an unusual and rare phosphate of sodium and aluminum. It is of only average hardness and therefore does not wear well as a gemstone. It does cut beautifully, however, and its chartreuse-yellow color and good brilliance make it a most desirable collector's gemstone. It was named brazilianite because it was first found in Brazil, and for a time no other country produced the stone. Then it was reported from the Palero mine, near North Groton, Grafton County, New Hampshire, and at Newport, also in New Hampshire. Brazilianite occurs in pegmatite veins and is associated with apatite, albite, muscovite, tourmaline, and whitlockite.

This perky specimen displays a fine-quality doubly terminated brazilianite crystal atop a crystal formation of muscovite. It is small as brazilianites go, but its crystal perfection, clarity, color, and matrix make it a winner. This 1963 specimen (just as with all fine brazilianites) was mined at Conselheiro Pena, on the Rio Doce River, Minas Gerais, Brazil. Much of the Rio Doce River runs between Governador Valadares and the Atlantic port city of Vitória. Not far from its banks hundreds of small mines have through the years produced a tantalizing array of gemstones and minerals, including tourmaline, morganite, rose quartz, aquamarine, andalusite, columbite, topaz, and, of course, brazilianite. There are much larger crystals of brazilianite in the world, and many of them are outstanding in quality, but most are either incomplete crystals or display considerable damage on the edge or face of the crystal.

Other fine brazilianites are in the collections of the Smithsonian Institution; the School of Mines, Paris; George Wild, Idar-Oberstein, West Germany; and Edward Bancroft, San Diego, California.

Nominated by Paul Fraenkel, Paris
Photographed by Mme. Nelly Bariand, Paris

RUBELLITE (Red Tourmaline)

Collection: The Smithsonian Institution
Curator: Paul Desautels
Size: 33 cm × 27 cm; 13″ × 11″

Tourmaline occurs in a wide range of colors, including blue, yellow, pink, green, red, and black. Occasional slender prismatic groups occur in which each crystal has two or more colors. As is true with other gem minerals, transparent tourmaline of rich pink, red, green, or blue hue is greatly prized for cut stones; its well-formed crystals are eye-catching in mineral displays.

The pink-to-red variety of tourmaline is known as rubellite. While the occurrence of tourmaline is widespread, it is found most often in black or brown colors. Rubellite is quite rare and has been found at Campolungo, Switzerland; San Piero, Elba, Italy; Pala and Mesa Grande, California; Antandrokomby, Madagascar; Governador Valadares, Brazil; and Ligonha, Mozambique.

As this page is being written, Edward Swoboda is working his Stewart Lithia and Tourmaline Queen mines, near San Diego, and recently entered pockets that have already produced tourmaline and morganite crystals that are among the best ever seen.

This example of bicolored rubellite is considered by many mineral experts to be the finest mineral specimen in the world. The green-tipped tourmaline crystals are nearly seven inches (17.2 cm) long and nest in a bed of flesh-colored cleavelandite crystals. The albite in turn rests on a group of doubly terminated quartz crystals. The specimen was mined in the Tourmaline King mine at Pala, California, in the year 1907. It found its way to the Smithsonian Institution shortly thereafter and has been a proud possession ever since.

Other fine rubellites are in the collections of the Natural History Museum, the Faculty of Sciences, and the School of Mines, all of Paris; the British Museum (Natural History); the National Museum, Prague; the Institute of Mineraology, Rome; the Moravian Museum, Brno, Czechoslovakia; the Institute of Mines, Leningrad; the Feire de Andrade Museum, Lourenço Marques, Mozambique; the American Museum of Natural History; and Harvard University.

Nominated by C. Douglas Woodhouse, Santa Barbara, California
Photographed by Earl Lewis

Geographical Directory of Museum Collections

The great mineral repositories of the world are the public, private, and university museums. These are the agencies which make easily accessible to the public, rich and poor alike, the marvels of the mineral world. The more important of the museums housing great mineral collections are:

Country	City	Museum
AUSTRIA	Vienna	Natural History Museum
AUSTRALIA	Sydney	Australian Museum
BELGIUM	Brussels	University Library Museum
	Liège	University Museum
	Tervuren	Museum of Central Africa
BRAZIL	Ouro Prêto	School of Mines
	Rio de Janeiro	National Museum
	São Paulo	University of São Paulo Museum
CANADA	Ontario	Royal Ontario Museum
	Ottawa	National Museum of Natural Sciences
CHILE	Santiago	University of Chile
CZECHOSLOVAKIA	Brno	Moravian Museum
	Jihlava	Museum Vysociny Jihiva (*sic*)
	Kosice	Museum of Eastern Slovakia
	Prague	National Museum
		Institute of Chemical Technology
		Institute of Geology and Mineralogy
DENMARK	Aarhus	Natural History Museum
	Copenhagen	Mineralogy Museum, University of Copenhagen
ENGLAND	Liverpool	City Museum
	London	British Museum (Natural History)
		Geological Museum
	Manchester	Manchester University Museum
	Newcastle	Hancock Museum
	Nottingham	Natural History Museum
FRANCE	Grenoble	Museum of Natural History
	Lyons	Museum Guimet
	Nantes	Museum of Natural History
	Paris	School of Mines
		Faculty of Sciences (Sorbonne)
		Natural History Museum
		College of France
		Paul Fraenkel
	Strasbourg	Faculty of Sciences
EAST GERMANY	Berlin	Humboldt University
	Dresden	Museum of Mineralogy and Geology
	Freiberg	School of Mines
WEST GERMANY	Freiburg	University of Freiburg
	Heidelberg	Institute of Mineralogy
	Karlsruhe	State Natural History Collection
	Mainz	Natural History Museum of Mainz
	Munich	Mineralogical Museum
HUNGARY	Budapest	Hungarian Natural History Museum

Country	City	Museum
ITALY	Bologna	Institute of Mineralogy
	Florence	Institute of Mineralogy
	Milan	Civic Museum of Natural History
		University of Milan, Institute of Mineralogy Museum
	Pisa	Institute of Mineralogy
	Rome	Institute of Mineralogy
	Turin	Institute of Mineralogy
JAPAN	Tokyo	National Science University Museum
KENYA	Nairobi	University of Nairobi
MEXICO	Mexico City	Natural History Museum
MOZAMBIQUE	Lourenço Marques	Feire de Andrade Museum
		Geological Survey Museum
THE NETHERLANDS	Haarlem	Teyler's Museum
	Leiden	Museum of Geology and Mineralogy
NORWAY	Kongsberg	Mining Museum
	Oslo	Geology Museum
PERU	Lima	University of Lima
PORTUGAL	Lisbon	Faculty of Sciences
	Oporto	Faculty of Sciences
SCOTLAND	Dumfries	Royal Burgh Museum of Dumfries
	Edinburgh	Royal Scottish Museum
SOUTH AFRICA	Johannesburg	New Library Museum
		University of Witwatersrand
	Pretoria	Geological Survey Museum
SPAIN	Barcelona	Joaquin Folch Girona
	Madrid	Institute of Geology
		Museum of Natural Science
		School of Mines
SWEDEN	Stockholm	Royal Museum of Natural History
	Bern	Institute of Mineralogy
SWITZERLAND		Natural History Museum
	Fribourg	Natural History Museum
	Geneva	Natural History Museum
	Schönenwerd	Bally Museum
	Zurich	Swiss Federal Institute of Technology
U.S.A.	Bloomfield Hills, Mich.	Cranbrook Institute of Science
	Bryn Mawr, Pa.	Bryn Mawr College
	Cambridge, Mass.	Harvard University
	Chicago, Ill.	Field Museum
	Denver, Colorado	Denver Museum of Natural History
	Los Angeles, Calif.	Los Angeles County Museum
	New Haven, Conn.	Yale University
	New York, N.Y.	American Museum of Natural History
		Columbia University
	Philadelphia, Pa.	Academy of Natural Sciences
	Santa Barbara, Calif.	Natural History Museum
	San Francisco, Calif.	California Academy of Sciences
	Washington, D.C.	Smithsonian Institution
U.S.S.R.	Leningrad	Institute of Mines
	Moscow	Fersman Mineralogical Museum
		University of Lomonosov
ZAIRE	Jadotville	Sengier-Cousin Museum

INDEX